Bill

Behind Enemy Wines
Olly Smith's World of Wine

Olly Smith

Cheers and Happy Tastings,

x Olly

First published in Great Britain in 2013
by Hot Bottle Press, Lewes BN7 1YJ

The right of Olly Smith to be identified as Author
of this Work has been asserted by him in accordance
with the Copyright, Designs and Patents Act 1988

www.ollysmith.com

A CIP catalogue for this book is available from the British Library

ISBN 978-0-9574480-1-8

Designed and typeset by Cosima Dinkel
Front cover photography by Alun Callender
Printed and bound in the United Kingdom by CPI Anthony Rowe

Behind Enemy Wines
Olly Smith's World of Wine

Olly Smith

Behind Enemy Wines is the second in the glorious series of Olly's Smith's 'World of Wine'. Delve in to find lashings of Olly's uniquely enthusiastic wine wisdom. And if you're thirsty for more, read Olly's latest wine thoughts in the *Mail on Sunday*'s *EVENT* magazine and sign up for Hot Bottle, his free wine email bulletin at www.ollysmith.com. You can catch Olly online and join the wine chat on his Facebook Fan Page, follow him on Twitter @jollyolly and learn about wine through his Wine App (imaginatively called 'Olly Smith's Wine App') which delivers all Olly's wine knowledge direct to your fingertips.

Thanks to...
Gordon Thompson, Andrew Davies, Gerard Greaves
and Geordie Grieg at the *Mail on Sunday*;

The team at *EVENT Magazine;*

My family.

Sub-Editor Richard Hemming for subbing stupendously.

Cosima Dinkel for designing this book with
the secret fingers of Mitzi Dupré.

Jess Hood for compiling these columns with élan.

Alun Callender for shooting me so painlessly.

Contents

Baby, it's cold outside... so stay indoors and open a bottle of instant central heating

At chilly times of year, wine can be deployed as a virtual duffel coat to insulate against the blasting winds of winter.

You might instantly be drawn to muscular spicy reds, which is a good shout. But if you peer a bit further into the cellar of stout wines, there are many fortified ones just waiting to give you the vinous version of a full body rub with Vicks. Think of cognac, armagnac, sherry, port, madeira and the sweet vin doux naturel of France.

First up, reds. There are a number of different ways in which spice can operate in reds. It might come from the variety, as in the case of peppery Shiraz, or it might come from ageing the wine in toasty barrels, which can impart mocha and coffee spice to the brew. You can even find truffly and earthy notes in classic Bordeaux and Barolo wines.

If you're a fan of bold, beefy red wine, the sort of thing that Brian Blessed would drink from a giant pewter pint mug, Châteauneuf-du-Pape is a perennial favourite made from a blend of grapes but heavily featuring Grenache. Grenache has the wondrous appeal of being big on flavour without being too heavy on body. It tends to have a subtle white pepper character and you can find it in southern France, Australia, or in Spain where it is known as Garnacha.

Carmenère from Chile is another dark, powerful red with spicy appeal. It ranges from more elegant styles to ripe, bold, big bottles that don't so much have labels as tattoos. You can find plenty of good value examples too. Grand served alongside a steaming stew of hot cow.

Port is a style of wine that too often gets overlooked. It's perfect beyond Christmas, into the wilds of January and beyond, to keep spirits aglow as we all scour the land for the first snowdrops and sightings of Bill Oddie free from hibernation. Port comes in a variety of shapes and sizes – my tips to you are to hunt out LBV (late bottled vintage), which offers great quality for the money with sweet, bold black fruit and spicy flavours.

Another delish port is Tawny – serve it chilled before a meal to warm up your diners. It's good to see port producers modernising, making projects with chic packaging and an accessible style for a new generation.

Port is also a great ingredient to deploy in the bunker-buster of winter warmers: mulled wine. A splash of port acts like stock in your gravy, enriching the flavour. You could also consider splashing in a dose of Cointreau – but remember not to boil it or you risk losing the booze.

Another fortified wine that could warm the cockles of an iceberg is sherry. Regular readers will know of my penchant for sherry be it dry, medium or sweet, and it remains one of the real bargains on the international wine stage. I won't harp on again about it, but do have a chat with your local retailer and taste for yourself. Whether it's a bone dry Fino or a sweet Oloroso, a bit of careful enquiry should sort you with a style to suit your palate.

And if you find sherry agreeable enough to warm you through and defrost your toes, madeira should be your very next port of call. With outrageous value and a wealth of styles, it's another unsung hero of the wine world that owes its unique flavour to being baked in a warm attic called an estufa.

I once tasted a range of madeira in a Turkish bath, and aside from being highly memorable, it brought a clear sense of the heat of summery Madeira harnessed in every single bottle. From dry tangy Sercial to fruity Verdelho and sweet Bual, madeira is a wine for those in the know.

Remember, the more powerful the drink, the less you need, so half bottles are no bad thing to keep your winter warmers in peak condition ready to build their glowing fortresses of flavour.

And if you can't find a drink to suit, you could always try hibernating.

If half used bottles of spirits litter your house, it's time to start getting experimental

Drinks cabinets up and down the nation are often bulging with brightly coloured and oddly shaped bottles. And as well as left-over festive booze, there's often a bottle or two of something brought back from a sun-soaked holiday.

So when I recently mustered the courage to rummage in the furthest corners of my drinks cabinet, I felt a bit like Indiana Jones exploring the ruins of some long-forgotten temple.I half expected a giant boulder to come rolling out and chase me round the living room.

Fortunately the most terrifying thing I unearthed was an unopened bottle of Unicum, a highly potent Hungarian black liqueur that tastes a bit like peppermint fused with liquorice.

Some bottles offer gentle, crowd-pleasing flavours – for instance, sweet, almondy Amaretto or creamy South African Amarula, which you can happily serve up over ice at the end of a meal.

But a lot of these forgotten tipples have more challenging flavours when served on their own. However, if you mix them into concoctions worthy of *George's Marvellous Medicine*, you can find yourself well on the way to drinks nirvana.

Starting with fruity concoctions, perhaps the most lethal is the appropriately named Zombie. This is more or less white, gold and dark rum, apricot brandy, pineapple juice, lime juice, sugar syrup and a splash of grenadine – but you can customise it with all sorts of tropical fruit juices. It's a poky drink, so it's best to garnish it with something appropriate, like a hand grenade.

A simpler fruity approach is to mix a splash of Cointreau with a jot of peach schnapps and top up with lemonade or orange juice. Or you could deploy the classic Malibu and pineapple for a taste of the tropics. Or go for a citrus burst with the Gimlet cocktail – gin mixed with lime cordial, ice and a lime wedge.

But for a seriously hardcore citrus tingle, reach a little further into the darkness of your drinks cabinet for the ubiquitous bottle of Campari. Campari is one of my favourite drinks and is hugely underrated – try a shot in a long glass over ice topped up with sparkling San Pellegrino Limonata.

But fruity is by no means the only path you can take when it comes to consuming forgotten drinks. How about a White Russian, made by mixing equal measures of coffee-flavoured Kahlua and vodka, throwing in some ice and topping up with milk? Or you could try Kahlua, vodka and Baileys in equal shots topped up with cream for an outrageous extravagance. Or there's Tia Maria mixed with cranberry juice and a slice of lime, which may sound like the work of the Devil, but offers a surprisingly appealing flavour.

Another route with spirits is to customise your own concoctions. You can infuse gin or vodka with sloes, or play with raspberries, strawberries, blackcurrants and more. You can easily create sugar syrups from fruit such as rhubarb (heat equal parts sugar and water until the sugar's dissolved, stew rhubarb, cool and strain), which works amazingly mixed with Prosecco as a cocktail.

For the very brave, try a Pickleback: one shot of Jameson Irish whiskey followed by a shot of pickle juice from your jar of pickled onions or gherkins. I admire the Pickleback for its double assault on leftovers in both the drinks cabinet and the kitchen cupboard, but I admit it curdles my mayonnaise just thinking about it.

And the ultimate option for highly stubborn bottles that linger too long? Cook with them. The possibilities include Baileys porridge, apple brandy in your apple pie, a shot of white rum in a lime and chilli salsa, vermouth with fennel, pastis with fish, pouring PX sherry over vanilla ice cream, flambéing prawns in Cointreau and soaking fruit in booze for all manner of dishes.

Or you could try my simple but highly effective homemade Baileys: a sip of cognac with a bite of Magnum ice cream. It's a total treat and might give you the courage to reach right to the back of the drinks cabinet.

Just watch out for the boulder hiding behind the Campari.

The ideal winter food: Stew.
But which wine to pick?

Stews are perfect for winter. These slow-cooking one-pot bonanzas with richness, layers of flavour and plenty of colour are the ultimate insulation against the damp.

But no two stews are alike. They range from bespoke masterpieces to fridge leftovers bundled together like the greatest hits of a compost heap. When considering which vino to match with yours, I'm tackling the four main types of stew: meaty, creamy, spicy and earthy.

With meaty stews, your ideal choice is a drop of powerful red.

Wine can be powerful in a number of ways, but for the kind of oomph required to match a hearty stew you'll want something with hefty flavour and a bit of body to stand up to the texture of your dish.

The cuts of meat you find in stews, such as braising steak or game birds in winter, are generally there because they're on the tough side and demand slow cooking to soften them up a bit. And that same slow cooking is what brings out oodles of rich flavour.

Grapes that have similar richness and body include Cabernet Sauvignon, Cabernet Franc from Argentina (look out for Pulenta Estate), smoky Pinotage from South Africa and Italian Nebbiolo.

Nebbiolo may be more familiar to you as the grape variety behind Italian Barolo, but although the wines it produces can be pale in colour, their structure and richness can be intense.

An alternative if you're a fan of Barolo is Greek Xinomavro, which you may need to hunt around for – try having a look on wine-search-er.com. Alpha Estate is well worth tracking down, producing Xinomavro on its own and as part of a blend. And Chile is a good place to find great value Cabernet Sauvignon, from producers such as Errázuriz.

Those enjoying a creamy stew, meanwhile, would do well to consider a rich white wine fleshed out with a touch of oak. Oak is less of a dirty word in wine than you might think. Like seasoning in a stew, oak can support a wine's structure and enhance the flavours. Grapes such as Chardonnay, Marsanne and Chenin Blanc take well to oak, which often adds complexity to the final wine.

If the label talks about 'new' oak barrels and the wine has been in there for 12 months, you're likely to notice a sweet, vanilla flavour when you taste it. But sometimes a wine might be aged for the same length of time in barrels that have already been used once or twice, known as 'second fill' and 'third fill' oak. These wines tend to feature a more subtle character.

I urge you not to shun wines just because they have oak in them, new or otherwise. Some of the finest wines in the world are oaked, such as Corton-Charlemagne and Puligny-Montrachet, and it's all a question of balance.

Some wine is fruity enough and bold enough to cope with a lot of oak, and it's the winemaker's call as to how much to deploy to achieve the right balance. If the oak is balanced, it should enhance the wine and help it pair with the texture of your creamy stew.

Moving on to spicy stews, these are a gateway to a wine lover's paradise.

You can tame the heat of the spice with a fruity wine – enhance the aromatics of the dish with a fragrant wine, emphasise the spice with a bold red or refresh your palate with a glass of fizz.

It all depends on the headline element of spice. My general advice would be to pick a red wine from a warmer climate with plenty of fruity flavour to take on the intensity of the spice. Think Spain, Australia, South Africa.

Lastly, earthy stews are wondrous for their complexity, and whether the leading components are funky mushrooms, sweet parsnips, earthy beetroot or pungent celeriac, a wine with a bit of age is called for to ensure a perfect pairing.

If you feel like splashing out you could sample a red from Bordeaux or, if you fancy a lighter bodied red, try a classy Pinot Noir.

Alternatively, for an affordable style of aged red that works with a wide range of stews, Spanish Gran Reserva Rioja can be an absolute winner. And with a hearty mutton and veg stew, it's positively sublime.

Chardonnay is much maligned, but if you won't touch the stuff, you're missing out

Ever heard anyone saying 'ABC' when ordering their bottle of wine?

Anything But Chardonnay is what it stands for. To me, that's a massive, catastrophic, point-missing shame. Imagine a Formula One driver saying, 'I love driving but I hate cars.'

Chardonnay is one of the most versatile white grapes on the planet. It produces bone dry steely wine such as Chablis, richer wines such as Montrachet and, of course, bubbly such as champagne.

Cheap Chardonnay can of course be vile, just like cheap Pinot Grigio can taste like licking a drizzly windowpane.All I ask is that we make an effort to differentiate between quality Chardonnay and dross.

If you've genuinely sipped a top class white burgundy or blanc de blancs champagne and still insist 'ABC', then fair enough, but if you haven't yet tasted a decent Chardonnay, give it a second look before you diss it for good.

Probably the biggest problem for the anti-Chardonnay lobby is the grape's negative association with oak. When a wine is aged in oak barrels, it can take on a vanilla-like flavour that, if overdone, swamps the wine and obliterates subtlety, elegance and complexity.

However, when handled sensitively, oak can flesh out a wine, add layers and bring out hidden qualities in your drink. Think of oak as being like a picture frame: you want it to support and enhance the central image, not dominate it.

In the Eighties, we Brits guzzled a massive amount of oaky Chardonnay, consuming it as an aperitif or a drink at the bar. This did the grape no favours. When the tide turned in favour of Pinot Grigio and Sauvignon Blanc, poor old Chardonnay got left at the door.

Heavily oaked Chardonnay was never designed to be an aperitif or bar drink; it works far better with food.

France produces Chardonnay in all shapes and sizes, but its spiritual home is Burgundy. The subtle differences in vineyard sites across the region send fans into twirls of delight. There are those who go mad for Meursault, who pine for Puligny-Montrachet and who go crackers for Corton-Charlemagne. Chablis has its fans, as does Pouilly-Fuissé, and you can find decent Chardonnay elsewhere in Limoux and Champagne, where it sparkles for a living.

It would be a mistake, however, to think that only France produces fine Chardonnay. Australia makes some which is amazingly complex and vibrant.

Alternatively, you can get a sensational glimpse of Chile's potential by investing in a bottle of Chardonnay from Limarí.

Then there's New Zealand to consider, with winemakers such as Mahi and Kumeu River producing terrific Chardonnay.

South Africa has some awesome examples too, from producers such as Ataraxia and Hamilton Russell, and then there's California – oh, and Argentina too. The list goes on.

You may think these wines are pricey, but compared to similar quality vino from Burgundy, they offer outstanding value.

What's more, even if you absolutely won't consider tasting Chardonnay as a still wine, I'm prepared to bet you're still up for sipping a crisp glass of bubbly. The grape goes into making fine champagne, certain brands of cava and sparkling wine made via the traditional method all over the world, from England to Australia.

So before you bellow 'ABC' at the wine waiter, be sure you've properly appraised its skills both as a blending grape and as a solo act. In some ways, Chardonnay is the Gary Barlow of the wine world. It's easy to forget the massive talent it offers, but once you remember, you want it back for good.

Yes, it's irredeemably naff. But there's no escaping Valentine's Day – so why not pop something pink?

Valentine's Day, no matter what you think, is romantic. Resistance is futile. I even proposed to my wife on Valentine's Day, popping open some fizz on her return from work, as I prepared to pop the question.

Nerves jangled. Pressure expanded in my chest. I gasped. I croaked and wondered why I was doing it on Valentine's Day. Aha! The reason I chose to propose on Valentine's Day is because Sophie would never expect it.

And I don't think she suspected anything until I'd drained a glass of champagne and started gurgling and wittering that I thought she was jolly special and would love nothing more than the honour of being her husband.

The fizz flowed, we made a phone call, my dad asked if the ring had come out of a cracker ... without question it was enhanced by the bubbly.

Of course you can choose inventive drinks for Valentine's Day but this year I'm backing a dose of pink fizz with which to woo. But what exactly is pink champagne?

Most pink wine comes from red grapes, with champagne sometimes being made from blending red and white grapes. The rule of thumb is that the deeper the colour of the rosé, the longer the red grape skins have been in contact with the juice.

Pink fizz tends to be pale in colour, a sort of peachy tint, the colour of pale summery roses. But pink fizz doesn't have to mean champagne. If you want to save a few bob, there's pink cava to consider, pink Italian bubbly, sparkling wine from the world over or for the patriots among you, English fizz.

With English wines, I often find a common thread running through both white and pink wines – flavours that remind me of our summer fruits and hedgerows, which can range from floral blossom to more zesty redcurrant zing.

The pedigree of English pink fizz is establishing with Cornish winery Camel Valley and Nyetimber in Sussex amongst others releasing some delicious examples.

For good value, Italian fizz can be superb. If your Valentine is a Prosecco fan then pink Italian bubbly can be supreme, with crisp zinging bubbly and plenty of fruity strawberry-raspberry freshness. Great fun, easy drinking and perfect for packing into the fridge if Valentine's Day turns into a party.

Or you could turn to cava for your kicks. Rosado can be great fun and good value to boot.

Or, for a wine made by the same method as champagne with the same grape varieties, there are some great Aussie beauties available – Tasmania has some fine examples, making complex fizz with plenty of ping made from Pinot Noir, Chardonnay and Pinot Meunier.

If it's champagne you're after, there's plenty of choice from widely available names such as Laurent-Perrier, Ruinart or Bollinger.

Or you could pick out a prestige cuvée rosé champagne, sourced from the very best vineyards in the very best years. Names such as Cristal, Comtes de Champagne, Dom Pérignon and more are out there with rosé offerings if you're hunting a splash-out statement bubbly.

Whichever pink fizz you opt for, if you find yourself in need of preserving the bubbles for a later moment, you're going to need a champagne saver/ pourer. That way, if you spend a hundred quid on a flash bottle you can make Valentine's Day last for a week.

You've probably driven one of their faultless cars. Now try some tongue-twisting German wines

Brits have a strangely close relationship with the Germans, whether it's over football, our Royal family, shared love of beer – or Basil Fawlty's uncanny ability to keep mentioning the war.

I'm a huge fan of Germany and the amazing wines produced there, but somehow, the perception of German wines seems still to be something reserved for wine fans in the know.

Sometimes German wine labelling can be off-putting, but once we get over odd sounding names, peculiar fonts and classification jargon, I believe that the pure, bright flavours of their top class white wines are an absolute thing of beauty.

For example, the Hochheimer Hölle vineyard in Rheingau makes magic dry Riesling. It's a heck of a name to read let alone say out loud but it's a white wine that should convince all doubters.

Shrill and bright with tangerine ping, beautiful honey-like fragrance, crisp and with fruit so fresh it feels like it's been dipped in the Antarctic. It is mesmerisingly tingly with a hauntingly subtle, exotic edge, and makes an awesome aperitif of finesse and supreme refreshment.

But apart from me, who's buying it? Well, more people than you might think. Supermarkets are reporting that German wine sales are on the rise. But that's not all.

When you take a look at specific price points, you find an amazing diversity of trends. For example, recent data shows that sales of German wine under £3 has dropped by 14 per cent – but in the £10 range, sales are up by an astonishing 204 per cent. *Jawohl!*

It's up to us as consumers to engage with the wine to really take advantage of the quality and value on offer from Germany. How?

For starters, winesofgermany.co.uk is a brilliant resource to get to know German wines.

There are stacks of grape varieties found in Germany, from white aromatic varieties such as Pinot Gris and Gewürztraminer through to reds such as Pinot Noir (aka Spätburgunder) and Dornfelder, but for me, the star of the German wine scene is Riesling.

First up, you pronounce it 'reezling' not 'rizeling'. It's a white grape variety that has a characteristic natural freshness and acidity that is sometimes balanced with a sweetness. It is easy to be intimidated by German wine categorisations, but if you want a dry Riesling, 'kabinett' and 'trocken' are words on the bottle that offer you the best bet. They can be so zesty and crisp, they're almost salty – if you like margheritas, you'll love these refreshing dry whites.

Spätlese is a style that is made to make your mouth water, with a squidge of sweetness but a gorgeous zing in the tail. Match it with mild spicy Asian flavours for a treat. Auslese is more luscious and for a proper full-on sweet wine look for Beerenauslese or Trockenbeerenauslese (also known as TBA). Both can be sublime with Riesling's magical ability to produce sweet wines that thrill with counterbalancing racy bright zing.

There's a German wine style out there for everyone and I was delighted to receive the following email recommendation from Germany's ambassador to the UK, Georg Boomgaarden: 'While German craft is often associated with manufacturing cars, it is fair to say that we put as much effort and care into producing quality wines as we do into producing quality cars.

Many German wines are naturally lower in alcohol, at only ten to 12 per cent, and there is one for every occasion: from crisp, bone dry Rieslings to Pinot Grigio or Pinot Blanc, as well as some excellent dessert wines.' Get stuck in.

Malbec: when Homer talked of wine-dark seas, this is what he was swimming in...

Malbec is a little like Robbie Williams: it has a career as part of a famous ensemble, but it's also a success in solo ventures.

It's one of the grapes that forms the blending recipe for red wines from Bordeaux, along with Cabernet Sauvignon, Merlot, Petit Verdot, Carmenère and Cabernet Franc.

Malbec has a reputation for producing beefy, deep dark wines. But that's not the whole story.

'Meat with Malbec' was the rallying cry of a successful PR push from Wines of Argentina, which tied up the Argentinian love of fantastic beef with the grape that's become their signature red wine.

It's a terrific idea and a slab of steak with a hearty Malbec is a magnificent pairing. But, of the many Malbecs I've tasted, one trend I can report is that where the Malbec comes from and how it's handled has quite an impact on the final wine.

Malbec is not just a fist of fun capable of producing hefty wine with more brawn than brains – it can also produce more svelte and elegant styles.

Cahors is a region in south-west France that produces the famous 'black wine of Cahors'. Have a look at cahorsmalbec. com if you want to find out more. You can find a few examples on the shelves of our UK supermarkets.

It's a chewy and savoury style of red with plenty of body and some serious muscle. One to match with hearty dishes like a massive slice of meaty pie served at the Annual Ogres Weightlifting Convention.

Or you could go to the other extreme and experiment with Malbec's fruitier side by sampling a Malbec rosé. Malbec rosé from New Zealand's Esk Valley, for example, could be a fruity, gluggable candidate.

But Argentina is the place where Malbec has really started motoring.

Generally in Argentina the grapes from lower altitudes seem to produce bigger, more powerful wines, while the vineyards higher up in the Andes can embrace a more elegant style, often with plenty of fragrance that I find completely glorious. Achaval Ferrer is a winery whose Malbec often feels tinged with perfume.

O Fournier is another Argentinian producer of fine Malbec in a winery that has some seriously striking architecture – think helipad meets spaceport in a mountain lair. It's run by the human dynamo, José Manuel Ortega Gil-Fournier, and on a visit to the winery I was struck by his determination and resolve to produce world-class wine. You can find his wines in Waitrose or by hunting on the very useful website, wine-searcher.com. For me, Argentina remains the place to hunt fine Malbec.

But watch this space. New Zealand, Chile and South Africa are all showing some promise when it comes to handling Malbec. Mostly you'll find it in blends – or you might find it by its other name, Cot, from Chile.

And of course, you could turn to Bordeaux for a classic jot of Malbec in your savoury blend, or turn to the might of Australia for a fruity, powerful blend.

Whichever way your Malbec hunt leads you, remember you don't have to spend a fortune to enjoy a young, fruity Malbec that's ready to drink – but if you do splash out on a more traditional wine with some chunky structure, remember either to leave it under the stairs for a year or two, or decant it into a jug a few hours in advance of serving it.

And it might help to serve it alongside a slab of mighty meat.

A cognac for après ski, a Shiraz for watching *Predator*… there's a drink for every occasion

I believe that a really great meal isn't just about what you eat, but where you eat it. Sharing good food and drink with the right blend of people in the perfect setting can enhance your eating and drinking immeasurably.

Supper clubs are springing up all over the place. It's brilliant to see the birth of a fun new dining experience that embraces a sense of adventure and experimentation.

And it's an idea about eating and drinking that has become my passion, as anyone who's seen my Channel 4 series *The Secret Supper Club* will know.

But does tasting a chilled glass of crisp white Muscadet, with its saline tint, improve by the seaside? And does an aged glass of red Burgundy taste better when sipped in an old leather chair?

Even with wine alone, setting has a huge impact. The bubbles in fizz are affected by altitude, and the biodynamic calendar also suggests there are good and bad days to enjoy wine.

One of my most memorable tastings ever was deep underground in a Hungarian wine cellar. Tokaji (you pronounce it tock-eye) is no ordinary sweet wine.

Finely balanced with sweetness and acidity, it's as thrilling to me today as an Opal Fruit was at the age of six. The deep winding cellars in the Tokaji region are clad in a black velvety fungus known as 'cladosporium cellare'. In fact, several Hungarian winemakers I spoke to insist that this velvety fungus helps maintain the correct level of humidity for ageing the wines.

Tasting fine sweet wines by candlelight in cellars of creeping black mould amped up the atmosphere and also helped unpick the riddle of why the wines of Tokaji taste the way they do.

But is there a wider call for wine to be matched with the setting?

Well, you're unlikely to pour yourself a glass of hearty vintage port on a tropical beach if there are lashings of chilled Sauvignon Blanc glistening in a nearby ice bucket.

And there are some traditional wine-to-moment matches: fizz remains the vino of choice to kick off a wedding; and you're more likely to find mulled wine at Christmas time than you are on Midsummer's Eve.

After a day on the slopes skiing, I swear by a glass of cognac – it unthaws and gently warms the human body from the tiptoes to the eyebrows and beyond. Check out brandyclassics.com for a brilliant selection of après ski tipples.

And in the summertime, every picnic should be graced with a chilled bottle of frothy, grapey, sparkling Moscato, with its fruity, crowd pleasing flavours and lunchtime-friendly low alcohol.

In the spirit of fun, I've been experimenting with matching wines to all sorts – books, sporting events, albums and even films. Oh yes, I find *Predator* goes well with beefy South African Shiraz. But you can do a lot to enhance the setting of your eating and drinking at home quite simply. You can adjust the temperature, the lighting, the table dressing and, of course, the glassware.

I once attended a tasting of fortified madeira wine in a Turkish bath. The idea was to mimic the 'baking' that gives Madeira its unique flavour, which takes place in hot attics called 'Estufas'. It was a fun idea but I'm not sure a hot setting is the perfect pairing with madeira.

In fact, I reckon madeira is the ideal wine to deploy against the drizzle – it acts like underfloor heating for the soul. It's intriguing and tantalising that a little extra effort with setting and ambience could amplify your enjoyment of wine to the max. A glass of smoky Shiraz sipped beside an open fire and I'm in heaven.

One thing I've been convinced of beyond doubt while filming *The Secret Supper Club* is that in these tough times you don't necessarily need to spend more to enjoy your food and drink to the max.

By using a bit of ingenuity and making an extra effort to gather together a group in a unique place for a magical feast you can share the great local produce that Britain is increasingly renowned for.

Tall, slender, fruity and fun... isn't it time you made a date with a beauty from Alsace?

Alsace may not be the first place you think of when you're tucking into Asian dishes. But from stir-fry to Szechuan, the white wines of Alsace are a great match for mild spicy food and a must for any lover of fragrant flavours, such as Japanese cuisine.

If you're a secret sipper of jasmine tea, snaffler of Turkish delight, glugger of elderflower cordial or just can't resist polishing off a whole bunch of juicy green grapes, Alsace could very well be your wine paradise.

Famed for its white wines, Alsace pumps out a variety of styles, from crisp to aromatic, and is one of the few places in France to make stars of its grape varieties, which are named on the label. Pinot Gris, Muscat, Gewürztraminer and Riesling are the big four, which can attain the pinnacle of Grand Cru status.

But you should also keep your eyes peeled for Sylvaner, Pinot Blanc and Auxerrois and, even though Alsace produces more than 90 per cent white wine, the odd droplet of red Pinot Noir.

Landlocked Alsace is among France's driest wine regions with a mosaic of soil types. Fringed by the Vosges mountains, the climate is generally dry with a long growing season.

Alsatian white wines tend to have intense concentration and fruity flavours, and can be made into sweet wines, whether from the late harvest 'vendange tardive' or highly prized 'sélection de grains nobles'.

You can even find fizz, known as Crémant d'Alsace.

Influenced by its proximity to Germany, Alsace is a superb place to visit, a wine region with its own groove and wine styles. Take Pinot Gris: in Italy, you may know it as Pinot Grigio – a crisp, light, dry white wine. In Alsace, Pinot Gris is a gloriously opulent style of wine, still refreshing, but with oodles more texture, flavour and richness.

This intensity and purity of wines from Alsace is what makes them fantastic to experiment with food pairing – even with powerful flavours. My pal David Galetti, head sommelier of Le Gavroche, is a visionary as far as matching wine with food goes and he loves Alsace wines.

He suggests that 'scallops baked in the shell with ginger butter sauce can't be better with a Riesling from the Turckheim area; classic matured Munster cheese with a Gewürztraminer vendange tardive; or try fillet of gurnard, meat jus, ceps and bacon, matched with a Pinot Noir from Alsace.' Alsatian wines have a wide range of flavours, and the possibilities to match them with food are endless.

You can easily recognise the traditional flute-shaped bottles from Alsace and, if you're thinking of a wine holiday, the Alsace wine route runs for more than 100 miles (alsacewines.co.uk).

But what flavours can you expect in the bottle?

Well, the white grapes of Alsace all taste different, so it's a great place to start planning your campaign. Muscat tends to be very grapey – if you imagine the flavour of a table grape, it's similar to Muscat. Sylvaner offers you uplifting freshness and makes a splendid aperitif – if you're a fan of Italian whites you'll love Sylvaner.

Gewürztraminer is a full-on flavour – think Turkish delight, rose, lychee and spice. Riesling is much maligned but in Alsace it offers citrus purity and verve – I find fans of Sauvignon Blanc revel in a crisp Alsace Riesling. Pinot Gris is great fun in Alsace – think ripe pears, richness and sometimes a hint of smoky spice. And Pinot Noir, if you can find it, has that cherry tang with a light body and vivid fruit flavours.

You can also find blends, but generally the heart of Alsace is in white wines of a single grape variety, a land of solo artists presenting pure flavour. If you're a fruit fan, Alsace whites should be top of your shopping list.

Champagne isn't just for Charlies: there's plenty of inexpensive fizz to be discovered

I love bubbly. It's invigorating, celebratory and uplifting. But the price tags can sometimes make it rain in your heart.

If, like me, you adore your glass of fizz and are on the hunt for a bargain, you're in luck.

Quality and variety have never been better – and what's more, there are some ludicrously inexpensive examples around.

Take cava from Spain. That can cost less than a gin and tonic on a night out – for a whole bottle of bubbly! It may not be the world's most complex fizz, but it represents fantastic value for wine that's made using exactly the same bottle-fermented method as for top end French champagne. If you're stocking up for a party, birthday or wedding, it's a great place to start.

Spanish cava is winning me over more and more. The three local Spanish grape varieties, Macabeo, Xarel-lo and Parellada, create uniquely crisp, apple-infused wines, sometimes with a funky twist. And recent changes in the law have permitted international grape varieties such as Chardonnay and Pinot Noir to be deployed as well (two grapes used in making champagne).

On a recent trip to Penedès in Spain, the winemakers I spoke to were keen to highlight cava not as a bargain alternative to champagne, but as a choice in its own right with its own unique appeal.

I'm a fan of the crispness of cava made in a modern, pure zingy style, and there are plenty of palatable options on the shelves.

Big brand names are worth digging into, as well as various supermarket own label offerings. You could even sample a delicious rosé cava for an early taste of summertime fun.

Prosecco from Italy is another terrific option, and with its fruity freshness it's a great aperitif which you can serve chilled or even customise with fruit cordials and purées to create your own signature cocktails.

Prosecco is not designed to be the world's most complex wine. It's created to be fun fizz and made via the 'tank method' (as opposed to the traditional method, in which each individual bottle undergoes a separate secondary fermentation). While there's a little less finesse to the bubbles, prices are good and the wine has a fresh fruity flavour.

But Italy has more to offer than just Prosecco. I think Asti Spumante can be a hugely entertaining wine, with its frothy, gluggable sweetness and low alcohol content – usually around 7.5 per cent. It's a surprising crowd pleaser, which may be out of fashion, but remains cracking value. Look out for Moscato d'Asti, a semi-sparkling wine that'll remind you of sucking fizzy sweets as a kid.

New Zealand makes amazing kit in the form of Lindauer, sensational value traditional method bubbly that's hard to beat on price. There's also oodles of sparkling wine from South Africa.

Limoux in France makes top flight fizz too, and for an alternative to champagne, look for 'Crémant' on the label. It's made via the same method, just outside of the Champagne region with a range of different grape varieties.

If you're a fan of French champagne, my top tip is to consider buying own label from the supermarket. They all have a decent range.

But if you really want to save some money and enjoy some bubbles, whisper it if you dare... spritzer, anybody?

These wines won't bring on the heat of heartburn – but they're still hot stuff

The dawning realisation that heartburn has once again snuck up on you to boil your guts is a bit like arriving home to find the dog wearing your slippers and ordering you to fetch the paper.

It's an uncomfortable, daunting and downright depressing state of affairs. When Messrs Gaviscon and Rennie have skipped town and headed off for a weekend break in the sun together, there are few things that can offer comfort.

Some say eat toothpaste. Others suggest a glass of water. I say, take a look at the root cause and avoid it happening again. And if wine is a contributing factor, think carefully before buying your next bottle.

What are the factors that affect heartburn? I'm no doctor but some say high levels of alcohol are to blame, while others point the finger at too much food generally, excessive amounts of coffee and tea, and zingy sauces and dressings.

But I think poor quality vino can't help, so my first suggestion is: don't drink plonk. You don't need to spend a fortune but if you're pouring battery acid into yourself, the odds of heartburn must surely increase.

Acidity is also a factor in wine that's worth knowing about. Acidity is a natural component, the zingy part of whites and a necessary edge in reds. If heartburn is an unfortunate recurrence in your life then you should consider avoiding grape varieties that have a natural sharpness, such as the ubiquitous Sauvignon Blanc.

Among reds, Barbera from Italy is a grape variety that I adore – but if heartburn is at stake, consider an alternative. Pinot Noir is another wine that you should probably steer clear of.

The great news is that there are plenty of red and white grapes that are more mellow, that offer round, juicy flavours without the flush of zing that can sometimes trigger an acid bath in your tummy.

The Rhône valley in France is a place that I recommend to those looking for white wines to avoid heartburn. The grape varieties that you find there tend to be round and supple – Marsanne, Roussanne and even Viognier.

You might also have a look at French white wine from Collioure, blended from grapes such as Grenache Blanc (low in acidity) and Grenache Gris. These whites tend to have an appley tint without being too aggressive.

Alsace is also a place in France to look at more luscious fruity wine styles with grapes such as Pinot Gris and Muscat. Gewürztraminer might also be a good bet as it tends to produce fleshy and exotic white wines with a spicy rose-fuelled fragrance.

You can find it from Alsace, Germany, Italy, New Zealand, Chile and beyond.

As for red wines, there's plenty to choose from. Grenache (also known as Garnacha in Spain) and Merlot are good bets. Both Grenache and Merlot are also found in blends – Rioja and Bordeaux respectively.

And how about port? Port has a high degree of alcohol, which may upset some, but its round and mellow fruitiness is often low in acid and could be worth experimenting with.

Indeed, curing heartburn seems to me a magnificent reason to taste some new grape varieties that you haven't tried before. Go on, have a rummage.

You've got the vino, the guests are here... but have you got the right glasses?

Washing up wine glasses is a task that requires concentration, a steady hand and attention to detail – none of which are compatible with even the mildest of hangovers. Some say only use hot water. Some say soap is the key. Others insist that white wine vinegar is the only appropriate cleaner.

And as for drying them? If you leave your glasses upside down on a dishcloth you risk a musty odour around the rim; if you leave residual soap in the glass it'll kill the next wine you drink. Some deploy a hairdryer to dry the glass, others a microfibre glass cloth.

You may think this is all a bit pernickety, but trust me, wine glasses are amazing at picking up odours – try smelling a wine glass that's been stored in a cardboard box.

I always smell my empty wine glasses before serving, and if necessary give them a rinse. With your wine potentially at risk, it's worth paying a bit of attention to the glass.

Anyone who's ever strolled into a big department store will know there are thousands of different glasses to choose from, so here's what you need to know:

Frosted or coloured glasses are out – you want to see the wine in the glass, not just for aesthetics, but also to get an idea of the condition it's in and its age (young reds are purple, old reds are rust coloured).

I use flutes for champagne – avoid the old-fashioned Marie

Antoinette glasses (the flat ones), as they give the wine a bigger surface area, encouraging your fizz to go flatter and dispersing aromas.

For reds the tradition is to go for larger glasses, and for whites usually smaller glasses. Think of them as like speakers – tinny little speakers are fine for treble, but for bass enhancement you need some big subwoofers.

Whether you're drinking fizz, red or white, stems are handy to hold on to to avoid leaving fingerprints on the bowls and also, with white and fizz, to prevent your hand from warming up the liquid. Try to avoid very thick wine glasses, as they can get in the way of the wine and dominate the sensation in your mouth – remember that the texture of wine can be as important as flavour and aroma. I prefer a very thin glass that gives the illusion of disappearing and makes it all about the wine, not the vessel. The bowl should gently taper inwards at the top to focus the aromas.

You can even tailor each glass to match specific styles of wine or grape varieties. Riedel has taken the ball and run with this and has a wine glass for pretty much any wine you can think of.

But there are plenty of other good wine glass manufacturers out there, from Dartington to Schott Zwiesel. I rate the Austrian company Zalto particularly highly. Its glasses are delicate and elegant to hold, and beautifully designed for enjoying wine. The one that catches my eye is the Universal glass, which is designed for both red and white wine.

Now, you may think this sounds odd, but testing the glass led me to buy a whole bundle of them. And I've even designed my very own wine glass to take this concept one step further.

My mate and glassware expert Daniel Primack always advises spending about the same amount on a glass as you would on a decent bottle of wine – the thinking being that investing in decent glassware will enhance your enjoyment of many future bottles of wine.

For me, the sense of balance in a glass is absolutely key. Any glass you buy should feel evenly weighted in your hand. The occasion is another factor. Choose fine stems for elegant dining, or perhaps stemless glasses if you're going to be sitting on the lawn for a picnic (they're less likely to tip over on the grass).

As for decanters, you can use any old jug or a fine piece of crystal glass – the idea is just to let the air get to the wine, which unleashes its full potential. You can remove sediment from older wines by using a filter funnel.

A decanter is also a useful way of removing snobbery – with no labels to judge the bottle by, you can just let the wine do the talking.

If sweet wine calls to mind the cursed spirit of Blue Nun, take another sip

Sweet wines, or 'stickies', as they're known in the trade, have a few diehard fans, but I believe that legions of undiscovered fans are waiting in the wings.

In brief, a sweet wine is created when the grapes are left to hang on the vine for longer than usual, which concentrates flavour and sweetness.

There are various styles, flavours and degrees of sweetness, but for me sweet wines are at their best when matched with the right food.

Even a good value sticky is worth serving as an aperitif in small glasses over crushed ice. Great fun.

You may think sweet wines such as Asti Spumante are unfashionable, but think again. The sparkling sweet wines of Asti are low in alcohol and, served chilled in the garden with a fruit salad, their jubilant fruity flavours are a guaranteed winner with guests after a meal.

And how about German stickies? The sweet wines of Germany are well worth exploring – look for Beerenauslese or the highly prized and even more intense Trockenbeerenauslese.

Then there's France, which offers a wealth of sweet wines from Sauternes. If you're after a bargain, look to the more mellow pudding wines of nearby Monbazillac. Meanwhile, demi-sec champagne matches brilliantly with puddings.

Look out for Bonnezeaux, Quarts de Chaume and even sweet Vouvray too. With Vouvray, though, be warned – it's best to ask about each specific bottle, as they can be dry as well as sweet.

Your choices don't end there either. Australia is noted for its sweet wines, and South Africa has iconic 'straw wine' made from sun dried grapes.

The high sugar content gives sweet wines the potential for serious development of complex flavours over a very long period of time. If that sounds right up your alley, my tip would be to go for Hungarian Tokaji Aszú – it ages beautifully and is a world class wine that's still amazing value for money.

The sweetness of Hungarian stickies is measured in Puttonyos, generally from three to six, six being the sweetest. Sweeter still, though, is Aszú Essencia, which – if you can find it – is a once-in-a-lifetime treat. I once sampled the juice directly from the vineyard as the grapes were being harvested. Sensational.

But don't for a moment think sweet wines need to be served in dusty bottles laced in cobwebs to be worthwhile. Not a bit – in fact, some winemakers are pushing the boundaries to create vibrant and exciting sweet wines. Take, for example, ice wine.

Ice wine (or Eiswein in Germany) is created by allowing the grapes to freeze on the vine in winter. When the grapes are pressed, the ice crystals are left behind and the remaining juice is concentrated and divinely sweet. They are delicious, but don't tend to be cheap.

There are plenty of winemakers around the world creating supreme stickies that are fun and affordable. For example, from New Zealand or Chile.

Wines such as these have an impact on me similar to that of the magic potion on *Asterix*.

Sweet wine matched with food remains not just a treat, but a must for any serious foodie to experience.

You've scrutinised the wine list and nothing appeals... why not bring your own bottle next time?

I'm often asked what the most expensive bottle of wine is that I've ever tasted. But rather than taste super-expensive trophy wines, I'm more interested in hunting out the best wines in the world that cost as much as a round of drinks in the pub.

And as far as I'm concerned, Austrian Riesling and Grüner Veltliner, German wines in general, the wines of France's Loire valley, Chile's Elqui Valley, the hidden gems of Portugal, the value of Sicily, regional France, modern Spain... all of these can yield tremendous fun.

And as for Greece, well if you're hunting wines in a restaurant wine list, don't be afraid to sample it – by all means ask the sommelier's advice but in my experience Greek wine offers quality and value for the discerning wine lover.

Restaurant wine lists are notoriously tricky territory. There is usually a fearsome mark-up and a bewildering selection listed by country or price with little or no useful information that could help you pair up with a specific dish.

But things are changing. I believe every restaurant wine list should include basic information, at the very least the alcohol level; there's a huge difference between a frothy lunchtime glass of sparkling Moscato at 7.5 per cent or a hoofing great glass of port at 20 per cent.

And I'm delighted to see an increasing number of restaurants serving wines by the glass. All the wines I serve in my bar The Glass House on board the good ship Azura (and now on Ventura too) are available by the glass.

Carafes are a good idea too. It makes perfect sense to encourage diners to sample different wines with their dishes as well as branch out and enjoy a wider selection of the wine list. We've all experienced the moment when you want red but the person you're with insists on white. But with many restaurants now happy to serve by the glass, this awkward moment should become a thing of the past.

So what about doing away with wine lists altogether and bringing your own?

The BYO Wine Club (byowineclub.com) is the brainchild of Khadine Rose. The idea is that you join the club and a wave of the membership card will allow you to bring your own wine for a corkage fee to some of London's top restaurants. This is supported by big name chefs.

It's a smart idea that's fast gathering pace. But how about nationally?

The food section on wine-pages.com has a comprehensive list of restaurants throughout the country that encourages bringing your own bottle along with the cost of corkage.

It's an excellent free resource that's worth checking out.

It's always best to call ahead and check a restaurant policy before you head out there. And use discretion – don't take a bottle of £3.99 Californian plonk to a fine dining restaurant and always be prepared to pay around £15 corkage in a top joint.

If you form a good relationship with your local restaurant and sound them out, you may well find yourself drinking some of the best wines you've got, with the finest local food for a fraction of the normal cost. In these tough times there's never been a better time to get to know your local restaurateur and form an understanding.

A table filled with a feasting BYO clientele is better than an empty table.

Spring? Check. Leg of lamb? Yup. Mint sauce? Of course. But which wine?

Spring is that time of year when the British Isles are bursting with buds, the grass is lush and birdsong is in overdrive, as if our chirruping chums are engaged in an attempt to force Simon Cowell to give them all a record deal.

And there's lamb. Lovely lamb. We're big fans of lamb in this country, and though there are those who mock our mighty mint sauce, I think it's no coincidence that lamb and mint both spring up around the same time.

Lamb is one of my favourite meats to match wine with, because it offers a uniquely fragrant flavour, moderate intensity and seriously juicy texture. Let's seek out the best.

For your hearty roast lamb, be it shoulder or leg, the very traditional options are an aged Bordeaux from France or mature Rioja from Spain.

Red Bordeaux from the Médoc is usually blended from Cabernet Sauvignon and Merlot, and as it ages develops savoury flavours and soft textures.

Or you could try St-Émilion, with wines based mainly on Merlot. With its earthy, savoury, dark flavours, it's the business matched with a meaty snack.

If you fancy something a bit different, go for a Cabernet Franc from the Loire, served after 20 or 30 minutes in the fridge. It's a grape

I adore, with an aromatic touch and a jot more lightness than Cabernet Sauvignon. Look for Chinon, Bourgueil or Saumur-Champigny on the label – or alternatively, pick one from Argentina, which has some cracking bold examples. Those from Pulenta Estate are especially worth sampling, if you can track one down – try bbr.com.

If you're a fan of more fruity styles of red wine, look to Chilean Cabernet Sauvignon or Merlot, or both of these blended together. Errázuriz generally makes good-value Chilean reds that are widely available on the high street.

Or you could hunt for a red from Rioja in sunny Spain. The region produces all kinds of wines: crisp whites, oaky whites, young fruity rosés, gluggable fruity reds and deep savoury aged wines.

With lamb, the Big Daddy is red Gran Reserva Rioja, which comes to you already aged in barrel for at least two years and in bottle for at least three years. This brings a savoury richness that also comes from wines only made in the best years. For more information about Rioja, visit winesfromrioja.co.uk

Just down the road from Rioja is the Spanish region of Ribera del Duero, which is producing some very fine wines made from Tempranillo, the headline grape of red Rioja.

Famous names include Vega Sicilia, Pesquera and Pingus.

When serving lamb with a rich spicing of smoky barbecue flavours, I've had success matching it with Shiraz. You could try South African examples – consider those from Mullineux Family Wines in the Swartland, or wines from Marc Kent at Boekenhoutskloof.

If you're stewing your lamb or serving it in a creamy sauce, you could even try rich white wines such as oaked Chardonnay or a rich Chenin Blanc, or go for lighter reds such as Pinot Noir and Beaujolais.

It's worth remembering that, in general, minced meat needs a wine with less structure in order to avoid swamping the softer texture of the dish. But with spring lamb, my favourite approach is to serve it pink, pour a glass of glorious red, sit back and listen to the birds.

Toasting a big day? It's a great excuse to open some English fizz

The most important question about a wedding, whether it's Wills and Kate or your own nearest and dearest, is: what should we be drinking on the big day?

If I were picking the wines for a royal wedding, I'd have no hesitation in bellowing orders to royal footmen that nothing but English fizz is to be sipped from dawn till dusk by every guest, straggler, gatecrasher and dignitary at the bash. And I've just found a belter of a newcomer: Gusbourne Estate. Producing wines of zinging royal exuberance and classy delicate bubbles, Gusbourne is a name that you'll be hearing a whole lot more of.

English bubbly is fast making a name for itself – with the new Rathfinny Estate near to me in Sussex, success on the international awards stage for Camel Valley and Ridgeview, and the establishment of reliable producers, such as Nyetimber and Hush Heath, as well as smaller producers, such as the splendidly named Breaky Bottom.

As well as fizz, our still wines are coming on, too. Wickham Vineyards in Hampshire has some interesting wines, as does Denbies based in the heart of the Surrey Hills. But let's imagine for a moment that Prince William and Kate Middleton don't enjoy wine. I know, it's insane but try to imagine it. There are plenty of other tipples from Britain to sip on the day, whether it's a glass of brilliant British beer from Thornbridge, Rocky Head or The Kernel Brewery, or even my local brew, a pint of Harvey's Best.

But there's not just beer and wine to choose from — think cider, from the finesse of widely available producers such as Aspall in Suffolk, to all the glory of funky local brews, such as Palmerhayes from Devon.

And there's whisky, of course, or you could plump for the great British gin and tonic. Glorious.

But let's be frank here, at a wedding, royal or not, it's all about the bubbly.

It's fizz that fuels the toast and propels us into dancing the hours away to the sounds of Highway To Hell and YMCA. And the news for fizz fans in the UK is that our southern counties are proving interesting and successful places with the right soil to plant the classic grape varieties of champagne — Pinot Noir, Pinot Meunier (black grapes) and Chardonnay (white).

If it says Traditional Method on the label, then it's made in the same way as champagne. And, remember, our climate is only a degree or two cooler than northern France, so there's no reason why we can't create our own unique style of zesty fizz. We've got the knowhow and are able to train our own winemakers at state-of-the-art Plumpton College.

And whether you're a Republican, Monarchist or just a proud Brit, let's get together as a nation, swig some of our finest tinctures and toast the one thing we can all agree on — it's great to be in love.

Portugal's economy may be in the red, but its wonderful wines are in the pink

Before Portugal's economic meltdown, I'd already decided to write a column about the unsung gems of this unique nation, as I have an enviable stock of its wines in my cellar.

I've always enjoyed port, but I also believe that beyond its famous fortified offering, Portugal harbours some fantastic local grape varieties, from whites (branco), such as Rabigato and Viosinho, to reds (tinto), such as Castelão and Touriga Nacional. A must-visit website is viniportugal.co.uk if you're keen to find out more.

In recent tastings I found the Portuguese whites (which only made up about 15 per cent of the line up) a bit hit and miss. Vinho Verde can be a beautiful thing, with its sharp crispness, and there are quality whites to hunt down, but on today's evidence, Portugal is really excelling with reds. And there's one region that shines above all others – the Douro.

It's a mighty and rocky region, long famed for producing port. The first time I visited, the arid schistous soil reminded me of Mars in the Arnold Schwarzenegger film *Total Recall*. It's a rugged, unforgiving and stunning landscape – with stone walled vine terraces declared a Unesco World Heritage site.

Port is a drink I adore but I'm thrilled to see the region diversifying into producing red wine of mind-bending quality as well. Douro reds tend to have oomph, spice and a touch of fragrance, depending on the blend.

They range from modern reds through to bolder, traditional examples with wonderful lasting flavours, depth, complexity, impressive structure and power.There are iconic names and huge talents, such as Dirk Niepoort producing wines that will make your toes rotate in your shoes with glee.

The Douro, you see, is home to some stunning red grape varieties that go into making port: Tinta Roriz, Touriga Franca, Touriga Nacional, Tinta Barroca and Tinto Cão.

But there are also plantings of red Sousão, with its bright zinging quality, and Trincadeira. Higher altitudes also offer some comparative coolness and, intriguingly, have white grapes planted for a new vanguard of Douro wines.

Beyond the Douro there's plenty of fun to be had in Portugal's other regions. The Alentejo is massive (about a third of Portugal) with easy drinking reds and zesty flavoursome whites.

Aragonez (aka Tempranillo) is the star of the red grapes, so if you're a fan of Rioja you'll probably get along with Alentejo wines. It's worth knowing that, as well as Portuguese grape varieties, Syrah and Cabernet Sauvignon are also planted, sometimes appearing in wines marked Vinho Regional.

Dão is a place to look for reds of elegance and ageing potential. Or if you've got a sweet tooth, you could look for fortified and luscious Setúbal from the Setúbal Peninsula. You could also taste wine from the brand new DO region of Arribes.

Portuguese reds rock my socks, from value to fine wines – and there's never been a better time to get involved.

What? Can't fork out £4k for a case of Bordeaux? We have just the thing

Every springtime, the wine trade is buzzing with talk of the latest vintage from Bordeaux, with predictions of quality and cost based on barrel tastings that will affect prices in the months to come.

Wines from Bordeaux are some of the most hotly anticipated, traded and celebrated in the world.

Buying them en primeur means buying your wine before it's even been bottled and shipped – the idea being to pick up stellar wines before their prices bust the stratosphere.

I buy wines en primeur every year, usually for drinking rather than investment, but whatever your motive, make sure you buy through well established sources. Names such as Farr Vintners or Berry Bros & Rudd are good bets.

Bordeaux prices in recent years have hit record levels, with unprecedented interest from Asia – especially China – and elsewhere. The big five names are known as the First Growths; classified in 1855, these are Château Lafite-Rothschild, Château Latour, Château Margaux, Château Haut-Brion and Château Mouton-Rothschild.

You can think of them like clubs at the top of the Premier League – only with less debt and fewer rowdy fans – and expect to pay in excess of £4,000 for a case of 12 bottles.

The investment world hangs on the lips of a wine critic in the US called Robert Parker Jr, whose praise for a wine from Bordeaux can send the price skyrocketing. His influence is massive on wines that are increasingly being bought as trophy statements or for investment.

Ask yourself: how much enjoyment can you really get from a wine costing thousands of pounds a bottle? Save yourself the cash and look for the more savvy bargains – within Bordeaux and further afield.

First of all, what exactly is Bordeaux?

It's an amazing wine region near the coast of south-west France, with a relatively stable climate protected from the salty sea by a forest with a range of soil types (generally poor and with good drainage, which is perfect for vines).

Bordeaux is divided by the river Gironde and its tributaries, the Dordogne and Garonne, into the right bank and left bank, producing mainly red wines that are usually blended from a list of permitted grape varieties – Cabernet Sauvignon, Merlot, Cabernet Franc, Petit Verdot and less often Malbec and Carmenère.

Generally, right bank wines are Merlot driven, whereas left bank wines tend to be more focused on Cabernet Sauvignon. These types of reds tend to be well structured and are designed to age and soften in the bottle. Their flavours are classic, which is to say more savoury and structured than fruity and juicy.

If you're a fan of classic wines, the great news is that you don't have to spend thousands on top Bordeaux. You could try Chianti, which is enjoying a bit of a renaissance, Barolo and other northern Italian reds, the wines of France's Rhône valley, or reds from Rioja and Ribera del Duero in Spain. Portugal is a rising star for reds and in particular try the red blends from the Douro.

For more elegant classic wines, have a crack at the French reds of Burgundy or for a touch more fruit focus get involved with New Zealand Pinot Noir from regions such as Central Otago.

Bordeaux certainly has prestige and the prices to match, but in blind tastings there have been controversial results. In the famous 'Judgement Of Paris' in 1976, various top Bordeaux wines were tasted blind against wines from California, and the results gave victory to the Americans.

Similarly, Chilean wine producer Eduardo Chadwick has pitched his South American wines in blind tastings against top Bordeaux reds.

Also, top Chilean wines have all been performing extremely well against their French rivals. Fine wine from Chile isn't a question of if or when – it's already here.

On a mission to hunt down a great grape?
Fix your sights on Grenache

Grenache is one of the world's great grapes, but as with the first mercenary to get taken down by rebel forces in a war film, somehow we forget all too easily about the contribution it makes.

Grenache produces red wines with medium body and low acidity that tend towards fruit power with a subtle peppery twist. You can find modern fruity examples from the New World – Australia, for example – and tighter, earthier, spicier versions from places like France.

Part of the reason why Grenache slips under the radar like a stealth pilot deploying the Goggles of Invisibility is that it's brilliantly successful as a blending grape.

The Spanish know it as Garnacha, and it features widely in the wines of Rioja. The French deploy it as the headline act in their famously large Châteauneuf-du-Pape blend (up to 13 grape varieties).

The Aussies have come up with GSM, a blend of Grenache, Shiraz and Mourvèdre which majors on dark, warming spice flavours.

And in South Africa Ken Forrester is making a variation on the same theme. Grenache is one of the most widely planted grapes in the world. But how well do we really know it?

Well, not well enough, apparently. Recently, winemakers, fans, bloggers and critics gathered for G-Day – the Grenache Symposium – to show it some long overdue love. Big names from the wine world made the trip, including Chester Osborn of d'Arenberg in Australia and Randall Grahm from the U.S. These guys believe in the pedigree of Grenache. They love it whether grown in its heartland, the southern Rhône, or by the so-called Rhône Rangers of the US. No other grape quite matches its subtle, heady twist of red fruits and spice.

It's a decent option to think about when selecting a barbecue wine, as it's lowish in tannins (the chunkiness in a red that can dry your mouth out), so it works with a variety of textures, and its peppery edge can help accentuate the smoky aromatics of the barbie.

It's low in acid, so expect plenty of mellow, round flavour, but watch out for the alcohol – Grenache can be a real headbanger, with levels in excess of 14.5 per cent, so it's always worth reading the label closely to avoid finding the Helmet of Thunder strapped to your head the morning after.

In fact, Grenache is rather good for making boozy fortified wines such as Banyuls or red Rivesaltes. But you can also find it in more delicate rosés, while white wine lovers can enjoy Grenache Blanc and Grenache Gris, which tend to produce mellow wines – sometimes with a funky note.

Back to the reds. Châteauneuf-du-Pape – with big names like Beaucastel and Vieux Télégraphe – isn't the only French region offering great quality; the Languedoc yields some brilliant gems too.

You could also experience top pedigree Grenache by trying a bottle from Priorat, an area of Spain which hasn't so much caught my eye as eloped with it, along with my other eye, nose and tongue. I'm loving these wines for their sleekness, polished finesse and intensity.

Priorat, along with Rioja, bears the prized title of DOQ (the Catalan equivalent of DOCa), and is famous for its llicorella soils made up of quartzite and slate. Check out the brilliant website winesfromspainuk. com, which reveals the various classifications used for wines from each region. It's worth knowing terms like these to decode the label.

If you prefer fruitier styles, go younger, but hunt down the older kit if you're devoted to more savoury flavours. And remember that you don't have to shell out to enjoy good quality Grenache – I've found some superb bargains from old vines in Spain, for example.

Rob Chase, who along with Alastair Marshall is the wine buyer for

Adnams, is incredibly passionate about the grape: 'Grenache remains brilliant value for money, it cocks a snook at the more reverential varietals and their followers, and only requires a free and enlightened spirit to enjoy its out and out joie de vivre.'

Couldn't have put it better myself. Go on, grab a Grenache.

Like any colour wine as long as it's red? Perhaps you haven't tried these whites for red drinkers

Ever turned up at a dinner party with a bottle of white wine and seen your host's nose gently turn upwards, as though your feeble little white could never be as fine, complex and intriguing as a mighty, brooding red?

It happens more often than you might think. There are those who'd never dream of touching white wine, let alone presenting it as a gift – some fear its acidity could cause heartburn, others find it lightweight and still more find it lacks texture and depth.

The good news for those who usually limit their bottle hunt to the red side of the aisle is that there are plenty of whites that positively ooze complexity, richness and class. And compared to their fine red counterparts, they're often superb value.

I was once bowled over at a Majestic fine wine tasting by a Grüner Veltliner from Emmerich Knoll. Its texture was fat and squidgy, it shimmered with fruit, spice and aromatic depth, and its zinging citrus flavours danced on my palate for aeons.

While its £30 price tag may sound steep, in the world of fine reds prices of £50 and upwards are common for the kind of complexity on offer here. But are there really whites that can be described as similar to reds?

Well, it's tricky. White wines are made in a different way to reds.

Reds are left on their skins (sometimes with a few stalks too) to fatten up texture; it's where tannins come from – chemicals that dry out your mouth, like those found in an over-stewed cup of tea. Whites are whipped off their skins, which explains why texturally they're much lighter.

Whites and reds can both have their flavours and textures enriched by sloshing about in oak barrels, which works like adding a sprinkle of seasoned flour to a gravy – it rounds out texture and offers an extra level of flavour.

Red wine more often offers a sense of mouth-filling scale, especially when it's from warmer regions such as California, South Africa and Australia. Robust red grape varieties like Zinfandel and Shiraz produce wines with rich, dark flavours and meaty, warming spice. Some can be so thick you practically need a teaspoon to scoop them out of the glass!

The only whites that really achieve this kind of textural 'wide load' are Alsatian Pinot Gris and Gewürztraminer, and dessert wines such as Tokaji from Hungary, Sauternes from France and Pedro Ximénez from Spain – all of which may put off lovers of red due to their aromatic flavours or sticky sweetness.

However, there are other whites that offer a certain savoury richness – look to those of France's Rhône and Collioure, Australia and South Africa, made with grapes such as Marsanne and Roussanne.

And purely in terms of flavour, there's no question that white wines can have just as much intensity as reds.

Ripe whites from warmer climes, such as Californian Chardonnay and South African Viognier, can be bursting with fruitiness – and reach dizzying levels of alcohol. I've tried South African Viognier at 15 per cent, with enough oomph to floor a rhino.

But if red wine drinkers' palates are oriented towards the more savoury end of wine enjoyment, whites with a spicy flourish are the ones to scout for.

Take the splendid and underrated Aussie Semillon, which develops magnificently after a few years in bottle. Or the peppery Austrian Grüner Veltliner, salty Greek Assyrtiko, aged whites from Rioja, fine old white Burgundy, or Spanish Fino and Manzanilla.

You could try leading red wine drinkers gently into whites by giving them rosé, but I reckon it'd be better to hit them with a white so radically different from any red that they've nothing to compare it to. For example, a citrus-fuelled New Zealand Sauvignon Blanc, a snappy Aligoté from Burgundy or the crisp, dry whites of Italy.

But make sure you're buying top quality, or the wines can seem a touch bland. Go for top notch Frascati or Verdicchio with its bitter almond streak, or, best of all, shock them with a dose of chilled, shrill Vernaccia di San Gimignano.

At the top end it reminds me of plunging into a cold sea on a hot day, or having a shard of frozen excellence fired directly into your tender areas. If that doesn't grab a red wine drinker's attention, nothing will.

What's new in the world of vino?
Here are the next big things...

Here I am in a giant room with around 20,000 wines. I feel like Augustus Gloop in Willy Wonka's Chocolate Factory!

The London International Wine Fair is a huge date in the calendar. It's where winemakers, producers, marketers, PRs, journalists and bloggers come together from around the world to discuss, taste and get passionate about wine.

As ever here, the question on everyone's lips is, what's the next big thing in wine?

Everyone knows I love boutique wine from Greece, but at this fair I can find loads more to get excited about, and go hunting for fresh opinions.

Stefan Gerber from South Africa's Boer & Brit winery is defying convention by bottling his Chenin Blanc in 500ml brown beer bottles, with gold crown caps. They look fantastic, and the wine inside is good. But why beer bottles?

'In the wine market we steal each other's customers, and we're not growing wine consumption. It's like playing touch rugby with your sister. We'd like to take on beer drinkers and convert them to wine drinkers. Environmentally, the crown cap uses very little metal compared to the screw cap and cork, and it's a bloody good seal.'

Dawn Davies, the effervescent sommelier at Selfridges, adores Stefan's beer bottle idea, but for her what's hot right now is Koshu from Japan.

'I listed a Koshu white wine three months ago and I'm amazed by how much it's sold. People are also looking for aromatic varietals; we've seen an uplift in Gewürztraminer, Viognier and Chenin Blanc.'

I wonder if this thirst for aromatic wines could be down to our growing taste for exotic cuisine, and interest in pairing wines with our dishes?

Rajeev Samant, the suave gent behind India's burgeoning Sula Vineyards, certainly sees a link.

'We're seeing new wines not just from India, but also China, and there's definitely a big opportunity for Chinese wines in Chinese restaurants, Indian wine in Indian restaurants.'

Jedi Knight of wine Matt Stamp is visiting from the States – he was once crowned US TOP|SOMM (Top Sommelier).

'I'm really excited about Sicilian wines. Sicily produces more wine than the entire state of California, and most of it is quite bad; however, I think there are some really great producers doing some wonderful things on Etna. Etna is one of the up and coming regions in all of Europe; the wines are fantastic.'

Some trends, of course, are more predictable: Pinot Grigio is still hugely popular.

But Noel Scanlan of Southbank Estate in New Zealand, is adamant that the grape to watch is 'Sauvignon Blanc, more Sauvignon Blanc and more Sauvignon Blanc.'

However, broadcaster Nigel Barden is convinced our wine horizons are expanding. 'There's far more room for really interesting grape varieties beyond Cabernet and Chardonnay. I'm thinking of Albariño or Teroldego, for instance – but also, the Russians are coming! Russian sparkling wine is really interesting down in the deep south.'

Will Broadfoot, the fair's marketing director, is the man watching over the 25,000 buyers and producers mingling under one roof, and for him there's a dichotomy between old and new.

'The last 12 months has seen a resurgence of some of the old school – Languedoc is doing very well, Sicily is doing very well, and I think the consumer is looking for history and a story attached.

On the other side, we've got Brazil taking a stand at the fair, Russia, India, Lebanon, Turkey. These aren't yet high street countries that you associate with fine wine, but believe me, you're going to.'

The range of opinions is as broad as the range of wines at the fair, but there's one thing everyone in the wine trade can agree on: at the end of a long day's tasting, nothing beats a crisp, cold beer!

Diving into a marine feast? Here's what to sip with crab, lobster and other shellfish

Recently I bought a lovely old fishing boat called Wendy-Lou. She's a bit worn around the edges, but she rides the waves off the Sussex coast magnificently, and is just the thing for heading out on the water with the First Mate (my border terrier, Barney).

Fishing is one of my great passions. For me nothing beats the feeling of peace and concentration it gives you, or the exuberant hope that comes with a thudding tug on the line.

And the latest addition to my fishing kit? My very own lobster pot. Lobster fishing is like hunting in slow motion, and I always feel like I'm hauling treasure up from the seabed when the heavy pot emerges.

And what bounty! Crabs and lobster are both glorious – and when I pick up one of each in the same pot ('The Crabster', as I call it) all I can think about is what wine to match them with.

Of course, fancy restaurants with stellar wine lists can turn out decent lobster – but my favourite memory of eating lobster is when I was at the end of the pier in New Quay, Wales, filming The Secret Supper Club.

Mansel the local fisherman and I had caught the lobsters that morning, and Mansel's watchword when cooking them is simplicity. Some say cook them in seawater, others in salted water; Mansel favours boiling water with no seasoning at all.

When pairing with lobster cooked simply, there are various classic wine options, champagne being very traditional. But lobster is both sweet and salty, with a meaty texture, which allows quite imaginative pairing. Sommelier Costanzo Scala bravely experiments with lighter reds, which work with darker sauces that boost its umami flavour.

A safe match is Chardonnay – try Chablis for zing, or Meursault for a bit more opulence and a toasty touch to pair with creamy sauces (ageing in oak barrels enriches the flavour and texture).

For me, though, lobster is most suited to grape varieties that are round and fleshy with a subtle aromatic tint.

Marsanne is a real favourite, and the wine I served with Mansel's lobster was a Marsanne Viognier blend. It worked a treat thanks to its peachy flavour and rich, mellow texture.

As for matching with flavoursome British crab, Viognier is the grape I've had most success with. A curious variety with a flavour similar to apricots and peaches, it works well with gingery foods, but with crab it's amazing.

You can find top class Viognier in the Condrieu appellation of France's Rhône valley, and good value examples across southern France (Laurent Miquel makes ace Viognier.) Chile, too, is coming up with quality kit, from wineries such as Anakena and Cono Sur.

Alternatively, if oysters are on the menu, a crisp chilled white (Italian is a good bet) or Blanc de Blancs champagne will see you right. Or you could opt for a surprising combination and try a light beer.

At London's Quilon recently I was served a starter of spiced stir-fried oysters paired with a wheat ale from Chicago. It worked a treat, as the beer is crisp and light enough not to swamp the delicate oyster taste, but with just enough flavour to take on the mild spicing.

Another absolutely classic shellfish serving suggestion is mussels with Muscadet. Muscadet was big in the Eighties, and it's still a winning white for me with its briny, salty freshness.

Look out for Muscadet 'Sur Lie', which has a bit more complexity and oomph.

And if you like Muscadet, you'll love the lesser known Picpoul de Pinet from southern France – similarly crisp and breezy and my top pick to match with bouillabaisse. It's a superb all round choice with shellfish, and still a relative bargain, with plenty at around six or seven quid.

As for the ever popular scallops, Austrian Grüner Veltliner is the wine I love to match, and for garlicky prawns or paella in a summery setting, I'm backing rosé from Provence.

And my tipple of choice on board Wendy-Lou?

A Thermos of hot tea just can't be beat.

Still lugging bottles out of the shops?
Then try buying your wine on the web

With the vanishing of familiar high street wine chains, the internet offers an incredible opportunity to find great deals, learn about wine and broaden your palate.

One of the biggest attractions for me is that hunting wine online allows you to research your purchase in depth from the comfort of your armchair.

Wine retailers are getting better at giving us as much information as possible online to browse at leisure.

You've got more than just a label to guide you online: there are videos and winery websites, and you can discover more about wine across the world, grape varieties, compare prices to get the best deals and plan the perfect food pairing for your chosen bottle.

You can even search a worldwide range of stockists for any wine with the excellent free service from wine-searcher.com

Delivery charges vary. Most websites specify a minimum number of bottles (usually 12) or a minimum value for your order. Look at waitrosewine.com and majestic.co.uk, which offers some great deals.

I can also recommend the wide range of services from independent online merchants such as stonevine.co.uk, leaandsandeman.co.uk or philglas-swiggot.com.

There are also specialist wine merchants such as vintageroots.co.uk, focusing on organic wines, or vinopic.com, whose specialist, Professor

Roger Corder, offers analysis of the wines sold, praising polyphenols but penalising high alcohol, sugar and sulphites. But does it make life simpler if you join an online wine club?

Nakedwines.com has an eye-catching concept using collective customer clout to strike exclusive deals as well as encouraging customers to leave feedback and exchange views on its wines. The site also promises a money-back guarantee on any wines you don't enjoy.

I'm excited to see that individual winemakers can pitch directly to Naked Wines' 175,000 customers, creating a meeting point in the market place between wine drinkers and winemakers. It's modern, it's exciting and I think we'll see a lot more of this.

But joining wine clubs is not new. Founded in 1874, the Wine Society offers excellent services and describes itself as 'the world's oldest wine club'. Life membership is inexpensive, with no obligation to buy and no annual fee.

There are other big names out there, including Laithwaites and Berry Bros & Rudd (bbr.com).

The *Mail On Sunday*, too, has its own wine club (mailwineclub.co.uk), where you can search under handy headings such as 'ethical', 'award winning' and 'special offer'.

But it's also worth checking out modern merchants embracing a spirit of informality as well as quality, such as planetofthegrapes.co.uk and swig.co.uk.

Of course, there are pitfalls with buying online and my advice is to choose a reputable seller, check carefully for hidden costs and always read the small print on delivery. If you buy a mixed case, make a note of which wines you loved to make it simpler to re-order.

Don't be afraid to ring the merchant before you order to ask questions and take advice, and don't be put off investing in a case of 12 different bottles – you'll save yourself the heavy lifting and you might even save a few pennies too.

Fruity reds to get the summer holidays off to a sensational start

What could be more summery than chomping on a punnet of British strawberries and revelling in their bright, intense burst of juicy flavour?

Wines can give you a similar thrill, if you know what to look for.

Of course, chilled whites are a delight to sip in the sunshine, but I'm also a huge fan of the glories of lighter juicy red wines with that summer berry tang. Lighter bodied reds are sometimes regarded as somehow inferior to beefier reds.

I once hosted a wine tasting in the Imperial War Museum, where I was fascinated by a comment one gent made to me when comparing a deep glass of Bordeaux with a paler glass of New Zealand Pinot Noir.

Both were spiffing wines, very different in character, but this chap couldn't take the Pinot Noir seriously, because for him it lacked colour and was therefore a poor wine.

But once he'd sipped it and understood that was the way the wine was supposed to be, he loved it – and acquainted himself with the rest of the bottle.

Pinot Noir is a tricky grape to grow, and at the top end can be very pricey and highly prized – I'm thinking of grand cru French Burgundy, such as Grands Echézeaux, Romanée-Conti and La Tâche. These elegant wines are capable of great ageing and develop hedonistic levels of aroma and flavour complexity.

But if it's a simple summery sip you're after, Chilean Pinot Noir is on the rise and can still offer some good value if you know where to look. There's some fabulous quality Pinot Noir in New Zealand – though expect to pay a bit more.

Italy, too, has a wealth of lighter reds to consider, from good value Nero d'Avola from Sicily through to sensational Dolcetto from the north.

Have a crack at some light, tangy Italian Barbera, which works a treat with tomato-based sauces.

For me, though, the top wine kingdom to search for summery reds is France. I've always enjoyed wines from the Loire such as Saumur-Champigny, which is made from Cabernet Franc.

Sounds a bit strange to say, but I love these wines' unique aromas, which are sometimes strikingly reminiscent of pencil shavings! Flavours tend to be dark and fruity with a punch of aromatic austerity, and they're good served chilled and have just enough structure to stand up to a plate of barbecued food.

You could certainly look to southern rural France for a light summery red, but the top place to hunt your light summery reds right now is Beaujolais.

It's part of Burgundy, and the red grape you'll find in abundance there is Gamay – typically pale, light and fruity.

In cheaper wines it can taste a touch edgy and tart. My mum has never been convinced by Gamay, and I think in large part it's down to the naff quality at the lower end of production. But when it's well made, from a decent vineyard site, Gamay's sleek, summery, perfumed, fruity wines can be striking and awesome.

The top wines of Beaujolais come from ten villages known as 'crus'. These villages – including Morgon, Fleurie and Juliénas – offer slightly different variations on the theme of light and fruity Gamay, all of which are regarded as being at the top of the Beaujolais tree.

You can find them on the shelves in the UK for a tenner and under. For a top wine from world famous Burgundy, that's extraordinarily good value!

If you haven't tried them, do have a crack at a Beaujolais cru – there's never been a better time to sample them while they're still affordable.

And yes, I will definitely be buying a bottle for my mum.

Bold reds and lush sweet whites... get stuck into the wines of South Africa's Swartland

The Swartland is a district in South Africa's Coastal Region traditionally associated with grain, but fast building a reputation for wine.

Named after the local dark 'rhino bush' (Swartland means 'black land'), it's a vast area north of Cape Town stretching along the west coast, and is home to some of South Africa's top winemaking talents.

Many of these young stars cut their teeth in big-name wineries before striking out on their own, and with a progressive approach to social media and an emphasis on fun, theirs is an example other wine regions could learn from.

On a balmy South African evening in December 2008, I first tasted a brand new Swartland Syrah made by a young couple starting out on their own, Chris and Andrea Mullineux.

The wine wasn't even in bottle and they didn't yet have their own winery, but it rocked my socks with its peppery punch, subtle fragrance, sense of balance, smoky, seductive depth and impeccable quality of fruit.

A year later, I visited Chris and Andrea on the day they were hanging the sign up outside the old hardware store that was slowly transforming into their winery in Riebeek Kasteel – a colourful, vibrant little town with a laid-back vibe.

Surveying the sign, clean-cut Chris mused, 'I studied to be an accountant. Spreadsheets and projections and precision are all I brought with me after my midlife crisis.'

So why risk it all for the Swartland?

When I contacted Marc Kent, the creative force behind Boeken-houtskloof and The Chocolate Block, to ask why he too was diving into the area with Porcelain Mountain Wines and top talent Callie Louw, his answer was snappy and simple.

'Bank robbers rob banks, because that's where the money is; we're getting more involved in the Swartland, because that's where the quality is!'

There's been notable success in the Swartland with grapes associated with France's Rhône valley, such as Shiraz, Mourvedre, Cinsault and Grenache on the red front, and Roussanne, Marsanne, Grenache Blanc and Clairette on the white. But there's also some fine Chenin Blanc around, on its own and in blends.

The Swartland also offers lush sweet wines with marmalade zip and sherbet sweetness – like an orangey, exotic pudding in a glass.

When winemakers truly understand their vineyards, I often find the wine in the bottle shines.

Renowned as the original Swartland pioneer, Eben Sadie is a wine-maker whose passion for his vineyards is off the charts.

At a recent tasting of his flagship red blend in London, he told me, 'the Swartland isn't the most known area in South Africa, but it defi-nitely has the most interesting soils. It's got no water, no irrigation and the highest number of old vineyards per capita in the country, and can produce incredibly high quality fruit.'

He's reducing the impact of oak on his wines, questioning why you'd want to make fruit from a 100-year-old South African vine taste like a tree from France.

A sense of balance and more elegant levels of alcohol are what he's aiming for, with freshness and a real sense of purity. Keep in touch with importers r-w.co.uk to find out more.

Su Birch, CEO for Wines of South Africa, is equally enthusiastic about the Swartland.

'New wine investment usually comes to Stellenbosch with restaurants and wineries. This is the opposite: younger people, not big capital, bringing back to life old vineyards and varieties which are either new or not usually treated with respect.'

With their pioneering efforts shaping the future of a wild wine region, the Swartland revolution is just beginning.

Yes, you are seeing straight – some beers were born to be adored by wine lovers

If beer makes you think of pot bellies and sandals, think again.

As well as being a magnificent tradition in Great Britain, craft brewing has injected a new lease of life into beer the world over.

There are similarities with wine, and brews can range from the palest of lagers that'll appeal to lovers of Pinot Grigio through to black IPAs that'll give fans of Cabernet Sauvignon something to revel in.

Beer in its own right is a smashing drink – and there's never been a better time for wine lovers to get involved.

A winery generally makes one vintage a year, but a brewery can brew different beer every single day. Craft beer is roaring across the US with small scale brewers creating new and vibrant flavours.

It's not a million miles away from Old World and New World wines, with modern beers tending to be large on clean, fruity flavour with intensity and complexity.

If you're someone who enjoys classic styles of wine such as Bordeaux and Burgundy, more traditional brews from Europe are probably for you.

But if you're a fan of fruitier and fresher wines from the New World, try new wave craft beers from places like America and Japan and from craft brewers in the UK using modern hops such as Citra (US) and Riwaka (New Zealand), which have a big impact on flavour.

Brewers can treat the water for each brew differently, adding a combination of mineral salts, and as with wine, the type of yeast imparts character, too.

Also, how much you roast your malted barley affects the colour of the brew.

With the simple ingredients of water, hops, malted barley and yeast, brewers have an incredible freedom to express themselves. BrewDog, for example, has been taking the world by storm with its nonconformist beers such as Royal Virility Performance and the 32 per cent Tactical Nuclear Penguin.

Home brewing is also encouraging amateurs to turn pro, a path that Evin O'Riordain has taken with the Kernel Brewery in London (thekernelbrewery.com). Together with Chrigl Luthy and Toby Munn, Evin is making some of the most exciting beers I've tasted, from his outstanding IPA brews to rich, dark stouts and porters.

'I worked for seven years at Neal's Yard Dairy selling cheese,' Evin explains.

'What got me into beer was a realisation I had after a trip to America. When we were selling cheese we'd know everything about it – who made it, the cow's name, the day it was made, the weather.

'America opened my eyes to the fact that people were making the sorts of beers that were deserving of that sort of attention and they cared about it enough to treat it in the same way as you would wine or food.'

Meanwhile, Willie Calvert, co-founder of the glorious new Windsor & Eton Brewery, couldn't be more upbeat.

'The craft brewing revolution has produced such a variety of different beers from fantastic new ingredients that it's become much more interesting than the wine market. Even wine bars tell us that!'

If you want to know more, blogs are great places to learn. The award-winning pencilandspoon.com is written by Mark Dredge, who urges exploration: 'Don't be afraid to ask to try before you buy. Any pub with a beer choice worth visiting will happily pour you a sample or two before you order a full glass.'

How we drink beer is also key. Miles Jenner, the affable head brewer at Harveys in Lewes, says, 'The perception that you can only drink it in pint pots is ridiculous.

'Beer is very much a connoisseur drink and you can easily match beer with food just as you'd match wine, with equal success and equal enjoyment.'

There are indeed some splendid beer glasses out there to experiment with. I'm a particular fan of the short stem Spiegelau Pilsner glass.

Beer's association with food has also been boosted by restaurants such as Quilon and the rising profile of MasterChef winner Tim Anderson, formerly manager of craft beer bar the Euston Tap.

If you're buying beer, hunt locally, visit your brewery or look online – slurpbeer.com has an impressive, growing range, and with the boom in brewing, it's only going to get bigger.

There's some mighty fine wine in them there hills. Saddle up, pardner. We're off to Argentina

When you're buying Argentinian wine, you can generally expect vivid wines with good concentration, fruity flavours and a bit of oomph.

But on my latest tasting mission to Argentina, as I sat hunched with my luggage in a prop plane the size of an envelope, I reflected on not only the size of the country but its vast range of wines.

There are some icons in Argentina – if you've sampled an Argie red, chances are you've tasted one of their mighty Malbecs – but trust me, there's a whole lot more awesomeness to revel in.

Malbec has become a hugely successful poster boy for Argentinian wines, in part thanks to a successful 'Meat With Malbec' PR campaign which linked their super beef with hoofing vino. Malbec is one of the blending grapes from Bordeaux in France and is also found in the so-called 'black wines' of Cahors.

It tends to produce bold wines with dark fruit character – imagine Rocky Balboa with blackcurrant biceps. Argentina produces stacks of Malbec and you can find fairly priced quality on the high street.

Beyond the juicy bold style of Malbec, there are further distinctions to be made. There are fragrant violet scented Malbecs, which remind me of northern Italian reds.

Wines like this tend to be defter, leaner and fresher than the beefier Argentinian style. But Malbec aside, is there more to Argie vino?

I've always believed so and have looked in the past to intelligent blending, unique grape varieties and good value.

Torrontés is a white grape with alluring lemony, elderflower and lychee aromatics – a top match with gingery recipes. Pinot Grigio has settled there, too. Bonarda produces juicy reds that are great fun, with cherryish bounce and a good bet for your barbecue.

You can find Chardonnay of decent quality from bodegas such as Catena Zapata, varieties from Tempranillo to Chenin planted by Familia Zuccardi and rich red blends fusing the likes of Malbec, Cabernet Sauvignon, Syrah and Tannat to rock your socks.

You can also find more unusual grape varieties of superb quality made by Pulenta Estate such as rich, peach-like Pinot Gris, or sleek and mighty Cabernet Franc.

But my mind was blown by Argentina's potential for fine wine when I tasted some Pinot Noir from Patagonia – it felt more like a two week trip to the Land of Glory than a sip of vino.

With complex aromas and flavours proffering layer after layer – from cherry, almond, raspberry, perfume, juniper, anise and an overwhelming sense of purity – this wine convinced me in a single sip that Argentina is able to make serious, fine and age-worthy wines. And believe it or not, it matched impeccably with fresh raspberries – as I discovered during some impromptu food pairing experiments.

Wine has been part of Argentinian life for more than 400 years, with more vineyard area than Australia.

With a continental climate, high Andean altitude and low organic matter in the Andes soils, it has a wild north-south range of diverse climates and regions to grow grapes.

From the rooftop of the world with pristine snow-melt to the rivers of the sweeping south, it's a terrific country and I couldn't be more excited by the wines of the future.

For value and stunning fruity flavour, Viognier is just peachy

Ask yourself: do I like peaches and cream? Am I an adorer of the apricot?

If the answer is yes, then hurrah – Viognier is here.

I adore it, and if you're a fan of mild aromatic wines such as Chenin Blanc, Fiano or even peachy styles of Chardonnay, then I think you're going to love it too.

With its floral aromas and flavours that are super-summery and embrace the spirit of peaches and apricots, it's a grape that makes me feel like lounging in a hammock and putting the phone on mute.

Viognier can produce everyday gluggers as well as stunning fine wine, but overall I think it's underrated and hasn't quite had the heyday it so richly deserves. Perhaps this is partly because it's somewhat tricky to grow and doesn't have a great reputation for ageing well. This doesn't bother me personally, as I love the fruit and fragrance this unique, mildly aromatic grape offers in its youth.

Its spiritual home is in France's northern Rhône, close to the town of Vienne, in an appellation called Condrieu and also Château-Grillet, a single estate appellation bottling top notch examples.

I shared a bottle recently with Saturday Kitchen producer James Winter – it was delish! We're talking a whirl of fragrance, apricot with a savoury dimension and a pristine, fresh finish – sensational paired with starters of prawns in garlic and crispy squid.

I've always loved the finesse and value fine Viognier such as Condrieu can offer on restaurant wine lists in comparison to, say, the top white wines of Burgundy, and I find it complements everything from salty shellfish (it's fab with crab) to mild spicy dishes, aromatic ingredients and even Japanese cuisine.

And it's famously awesome paired with turbot. Or how about served with a buttery roast chicken laced with thyme and lemon for Sunday lunch? Yes please! But perhaps the best thing about Viognier is that you don't need to re-mortgage your house to enjoy some splendid examples – and they're widely available.

Across the south of France there are some fantastic pockets of Viognier production, with top names such as Paul Mas, Gérard Bertrand and Laurent Miquel turning out spankingly decent vino that's available in abundance in the UK. You can also find Viognier in inventive French blends, with the likes of Grenache Blanc, Marsanne and Vermentino. There are also blends from other countries, including Australia.

For me, France is the place currently offering the most attractive price-quality balance – along with the widest choice.

The French have always had a discreet love affair with Viognier. In fact, they love it so much they even blend it with red wines – a famous example being Côte-Rôtie, where a squirt of Viognier can be added to red Syrah to bring out a subtle fragrance in the final wine. This has been mimicked by Shiraz-Viognier blends across the world.

I've also tasted superb Viognier from Chile, which you can easily find on the shelves. I've tried big examples from South Africa with such mighty levels of alcohol I imagine a rhino would be floored by the merest whiff.

There's some good wine coming out of North America too – but it's Australia where I'd consider hunting for Viognier with intensity, concentration and sometimes even a jolt of spice.

It's a pity that Viognier is tricky to grow, as I'd love to see more of it with different nuances from all over the world. Whether on its own or blended with other grapes, it has an unmistakable character.

If you ever smell a white wine and the aromas instantly remind you of apricots, grab it with both hands and celebrate the virtue of Viognier.

Sample some wine wizardry from an unsung corner of Oz: Margaret River

Australian wine – what does it make you think of? Sunshine? Good times? Shrimp on the barbie?

I'll bet you've sipped your fair share of big brand Aussie vino, and for many it was what got us interested in wine in the first place. I was drawn to them because they somehow felt friendly and easy to understand.

The labels were in plain English, often with food-matching tips, and there were widely available brands that could be relied on year in, year out to produce vibrant, fruity wines that hit the spot without hitting your pocket.

Times change, though, and Aussie wine has been going through a rough patch. But there's more to Australia than good value, bold, informal sipping.

The sheer scale of the country is overwhelming (the first time I flew across it I wondered if the sea had dried up, leaving the Earth like a giant dusty aniseed ball), and it has around 60 wine regions, offering impressive diversity and finesse.

You may have heard of Barossa Valley, with its mighty Shiraz, Clare Valley Riesling and Coonawarra Cabernet Sauvignon. But what about the cool climate wines of Tasmania, the range of styles from the Yarra Valley or the hidden wines of Margaret River?

All these areas offer quality with a uniquely local character, and for those in the know, some top notch wines at accessible prices.

The Margaret River region is a world of its own with a unique range of wines, and an area that I think deserves more attention. About 60 miles north to south and up to 17 miles wide, it's situated on the west coast, south of Perth, which is a four hour flight from Sydney.

That's roughly the equivalent of flying from London to Tel Aviv. Happily, however, if you're visiting from the UK you can fly straight to Perth, then head down and get stuck into the local wine lists right away.

You may well have tasted a wine from Margaret River without even knowing it – Vasse Felix, Moss Wood and Cape Mentelle are some of the better-known names – but by and large it remains a place for those in the know. Slowly but surely, though, its reputation is building. Vineyards were first planted seriously there in the Sixties, and today it has over 120 wine producers (many boutique).

It may only account for a fraction of Australia's wine output but in terms of premium wine, it punches well above its weight. Take Chardonnay. For years Aussie Chardonnay was bold and lashed with oak, and here in the UK it rather fell out of fashion.

Today, I'm tasting better and better balanced Oz Chardonnay with polish, zing and finesse – and Margaret River is one of the places responsible, with producers such as Pierro and Leeuwin leading the charge.

Food and drink are closely associated in the region, and to my mind this has helped raise standards and encouraged the creation of more imaginative wines.

Margaret River is blessed with a Mediterranean climate, enabling production of reds and whites, which combine a sense of freshness with fullness.

On the white front, you'll find Sauvignon Blanc, Semillon, Chardonnay and Verdelho, all with their own unique personalities, as well as Sauvignon blended with Semillon, something winemakers in Bordeaux are famous for too.

And if you enjoy intense, citrusy Sauvignon Blanc, you'll love Margaret River's crisp, dry Rieslings.

Cabernet Sauvignon is the red grape the region is probably best known for, and you can find it blended with all sorts (including Petit Verdot, Malbec and Merlot), but there's also some noteworthy Shiraz that's worth saddling up to hunt for.

Quite a few wineries are also interested in biodynamic wine production (organic in the fast lane, following the principles of Rudolf Steiner), including Cowaramup Wines and the local legend that is Cullen Wines.

As a region that's comparatively small but blessed with stunning beaches, a beautiful climate and decent wine, Margaret River is well worth exploring. I'm planning to pop there for a visit this very afternoon – one glass at a time.

For a country better known for its music and mountains, Austria can turn out some blinding whites

Aaaaah, Austria. Alpine meadows, Mozart and *The Sound Of Music*. Splendid! But who drinks Austrian wine?

Well, me for a start. There are a range of reds and whites produced locally, but the star of the Austrian output is Grüner Veltliner.

First of all, how to say it: grooner velt-leaner. Don't let the tricky name put you off; it's an exultant white grape, generally producing crisp wines with a subtle aromatic twist.

If you're a fan of zingy whites such as Sauvignon Blanc or Muscadet, give Grüner a go – along with a sense of bright refreshment it can also offer round texture, which makes it fantastic to pair with a range of foods.

For example, two of the hardest flavours to match wine with are asparagus and artichoke. Both make wine taste edgy and bitter. But Grüner, the miracle grape, pairs up with them a treat. It's also stunning with scallops and can be magical with mackerel

But what should you be looking for to get that joyful sense of thrust and zing?

Generally, if you're looking for a crisp, dry Grüner look for Klassik, Kabinett or Federspiel on the label. Richer, fuller wines will generally be labelled Reserve, Spätlese Trocken or Smaragd.

There are many regions in Austria producing decent versions, including Kremstal and Kamptal. But one place that has taken Grüner to its heart is the Wachau. Set in the stunning Danube valley, vines were terraced and cultivated here by monks in the Middle Ages.

The area offers three categories of Grüner, all of which are dry in style but offer different levels of power and texture.

Steinfeder is a term for light, fresh Grüner with alcohol up to 11.5 %. Federspiel is richer, with alcohol between 11.5 and 12.5 %.

Smaragd is the richest and most opulent style, with alcohol levels above 12.5 %. It is considered the most treasured and age-worthy style of Grüner Veltliner in the Wachau.

Top producers of Grüner Veltliner are well worth seeking out, but a lot of really stunning winemakers are working with high street supermarkets to produce outstanding own label versions.

There's some serious wizardry going on in the hands of wineries such as Rabl or Birgit Eichinger, both based in Kamptal.

Another top producer whose wines I have long admired is Pichler, and you can hunt its wares using the excellent free service of wine-searcher.com – but be warned, you may need a fire extinguisher to put your wallet out.

Johan Donabaum is a young exceptional winemaker who is my hot tip for the future. Imported by class outfit Novum Wines, you can find Johann's vinos in local retailers.

But the best news of all about Grüner Veltliner is that it is spreading beyond the borders of Austria to make new and interesting wines. Recently I tasted my first Grüner Veltliner from New Zealand..

The sommelier who recommended it to me said she looks for 'originality and value for money. It's everything around the wine: where it's from, the people that make it, finding local grapes'.

And where Grüner is concerned, I'd love to see it spread like a chain of invigorating hugs around the world.

Who needs the sun when you could be chilling out with a zingy glass of vino?

The British summer can be patchy. But that usually means the best is still to come and soon enough we'll find ourselves bathed in glorious golden light, wishing we'd stocked up on fridge-loads of cool, refreshing vino to see us through.

I'm thinking of sharp, snappy whites, pristine rosés and even reds with some tang that you could serve chilled.

So what should we be looking for?

In terms of grapes, if you're looking for crisp whites, Italy has a jaw-dropping range of zingers. Italian Pinot Grigio is widely available and astonishingly popular – my tip is to look for examples from the cool, northern Alto Adige.

We seem to be drinking more and more Pinot Grigio, and its vineyards are spreading around the world from Argentina to England. But the truth is, Italy has a myriad of crisp whites beyond Pinot Grigio that offer stacks of character and splendid value for money.

Fiano from Sicily and Campania is amazing – peachy, round and refreshing. Greco di Tufo is elfish, bright and dazzlingly fresh vino. Verdicchio dei Castelli di Jesi is clean with a subtle almond bite. And Frascati is making a comeback.

Soave is extraordinary when it's done right. On a recent visit to the area, I tasted a wine that blew my mind with its quality. Part fermented in oak, it was an amazingly rich and zingy wine with almond, pear, pineapple and a long, fresh finish.

Of course, Sauvignon Blanc is a massively popular grape variety, with sharp grapefruit zing and different nuances around the world. In France, in places such as the Loire and the appellations Pouilly-Fumé and Sancerre, it has a light, bright purity.

And if you search in less well known places you can find great value.

Look for Sauvignon de Touraine – it's very similar to Sancerre but without the high price tag.

In New Zealand's famous Marlborough region, Sauvignon Blanc takes on a special passion fruit intensity with tropical ping.

And you can find some real class from Chile in coastal Casablanca and Leyda or high in the Andes.

South Africa, too, has some wonderful Sauvignon Blanc, from areas such as Elim and Elgin.

And closer to home, France has some wonderfully crisp, good value zingers such as Muscadet and Picpoul de Pinet. Spain and Portugal also shine with their Albariño and Vinho Verde respectively – both stunning, crisp whites. But whites aside, is there an alternative? Rosé deserves a big mention as a crisp refresher for summer.

Not the sweet fruity ones for me, thanks, but the crisp, dry, holiday–infused wines of France's Provence will do me nicely.

And, of course, if you're a red wine lover, look for lighter grapes such as Pinot Noir and Nero d'Avola and serve them a tad chilled. Half an hour in the fridge should sort you out and emphasise the fruity flavours in the vino.

And if the summer continues to be a patchy one, you could always hold on for the first bonfires of autumn and serve these chilled beauties wrapped up in a toasty coat!

Leave the sweet, sticky stuff in Granny's cupboard... and pair your tapas with a fine, crisp, dry sherry

I am strolling through the white-washed and charmingly scruffy southern Spanish port of Sanlúcar de Barrameda.

As well as being home to the lightest and driest of all sherries – Manzanilla – this port brings in some of the most unusual and delicious seafood I've ever tasted.

I'm heading for lunch with Javier Hidalgo, the man behind La Gitana Manzanilla. Breezy, tangy and crisp, this chilled, pale drink is about as far away from the traditional image of sherry as it's possible to get.

Sherry is made by fractionally blending barrels of different ages to produce a consistent style of fortified wine. This miracle of continuity is known as the 'solera' systems.

There are many styles of sherry, but if you're a fan of the savoury tang of Marmite or adore the salty hint of a bone dry Martini served with an olive or two, I reckon you'll love Manzanilla.

Sherry can conjure up images of sweet sticky bottles at the back of Granny's drinks cabinet but the two lightest and driest styles – Manzanilla and Fino – are leading a sherry renaissance among foodies in the UK. These are crisp, zippy drinks born to be matched with savoury nibbles. They are all about invigoration and their sole purpose is to polish your palate and enhance your appetite.

My lunch today with Javier is an odyssey of the ocean. I'm served ortiguillas (sea anemones), huevos de choco (cuttlefish 'eggs'), monk-fish stewed with local vegetables and the startling scuttling sea creatures known locally as galeras or mantis shrimp. The biggest eye-opener for me is how gloriously all these flavours of the sea work together when paired with a chilled glass of Manzanilla.

Manzanilla is made by the seaside at the mouth of the Guadalquivir river and the sea breeze contributes to its freshness. This crisp refreshing style of sherry is created thanks to a blanket of yeast known as flor, which rests on top of the liquid in the barrel keeping the wine bright and fresh while imparting a subtle bitter tang – think camomile (Manzanilla also means camomile in Spanish).

In Jerez, which is further inland, the climate is colder in winter and hotter in summer which influences the flor to create the more savoury tinged Fino. The nuttier savoury depth of Fino is an invigorating partner to a shared plate of cured jamón ibérico, green olives or bowl of salted almonds.

In Spanish tapar means 'to cover' and originally snacks such as jamón ibérico were carried on top of glasses of Manzanilla, and, so the story goes, tapas was born.

In the UK, there are more and more places to enjoy these light sherries with tapas.

The quality of sherries across the board is generally high with great producers like Harveys, Lustau, Solear and more to choose from, as well as a healthy supermarket own label offerings, including some which are intelligently delivered in smaller bottles to deploy as required.

And if you're already a fan of dry sherry, what other wines could tickle your tastebuds? The grapes that go into making sherry such as Palomino Fino and Pedro Ximénez are not often found outside of sherry country. But Pedro Ximénez (or PX for short) is enjoying some popularity, notably in Chile as a dry zingy white wine.

Modern white wines from Rioja or Albariño from Spain's Galicia could also hit the spot. You could even look to Greek whites for your zesty tangy vino, such as Assyrtiko from Santorini. Or you could stick with sherry but try something unique such as a single vineyard Manzanilla. Aged for a more savoury kick and served chilled, these wines make a sublime match for shellfish – try it with prawns drenched in olive oil cooked with chilli and garlic.

The watchword with these bone dry gems is to serve them as chilled and fresh as possible – as you would with shellfish. Please don't keep Fino or Manzanilla for months in the back of a cupboard like Granny. Enjoy them straight from the fridge... the sooner, the better.

Make an appointment with the wines of the Languedoc. They might even change your life...

I once went on holiday to the Languedoc, staying in a charmingly snug village near the glorious ancient town of Pézenas.

Well, I say on holiday, but as my wife knows only too well whenever I'm anywhere near a winery, I can't stop myself from sniffing out the finest vineyards.

And there's some sensational value on offer here.

I only wish there wasn't so much tax and duty on our vino back home as I'd love more people to know of the incredible value and wonderful charm that's packed into the wines of the Languedoc.

Vines have been in the Languedoc for thousands of years. The story goes that the Ancient Greeks brought them here, and I can see why vineyards have thrived. Thanks to the warm climate you can expect wines with decent intensity and plenty of personality.

In fact, a few years ago it was a wine from the Languedoc that changed my life and led me into my wine-loving career.

In the early Nineties I was a student at Edinburgh University studying English when I strolled past a 'free tasting' sign outside Oddbins on South Clerk Street. I was a student, there was free wine; it was a no brainer!

I tasted a wine by Jacques & Francois Lurton made from the Terret grape from the Languedoc. It was around £3.69 and it blew me away with its zingy, crisp exuberance.

I felt inspired – it was within my budget, something I could share with my mates and opened the door for me to think about what foods to match and, more importantly, the wider world of wines I decided there and then that I'd love to taste. And the Languedoc is a world of wine in itself.

Alongside good value regional wines (labelled either 'Vin de Pays d'Oc' or 'IGP d'Oc') there are splendid appellations that specialise in certain styles of wines – Picpoul de Pinet, for example, is an appellation near the seaside pumping out some top notch crisp whites that will dazzle the palates of Muscadet lovers or fans of Sauvignon Blanc.

I sipped lashings of the stuff on holiday – it's light, lemony and amazing paired with fish and shellfish. I had a sublime moment in the lavishly stocked fish market at Sète where a glass of Picpoul and an oyster can be had for a couple of euros. Brilliant fun.

You can find examples of good Picpoul de Pinet in most supermarkets.

But the Languedoc has a wealth of other white grapes, all with unique flavours, from peachy Viognier to aromatic Marsanne and even zesty Vermentino. Or if it's fizz you're after, Limoux has some superb offerings.

And as for reds, you're spoiled for choice with Pic St Loup, Faugères, Fitou, Minervois, Corbières and more offering good, honest hearty reds. With powerfully flavoured grapes such as Syrah, Mourvèdre and Grenache leading the charge, expect spice, hoof and fullness – perfect to accompany a barbecued meat feast.

There are splendid fortified wines from Banyuls and Rivesaltes and sweet Muscat too.

Besides that, there are superb quality bottles that I think of as special occasion wines, including reds from appellations with growing reputations for excellence such as Minervois La Livinière.

And there are even some good value modern brands to look out for.

So whether it's reds, whites, fizz, fortified, sweet or a summery rosé, Languedoc has got it all. Go get some!

Wander off the beaten track for superb quality wines at gobsmacking prices

You might think wine lovers only ever buy spankingly expensive 'fine wine', jumping on the Bordeaux bandwagon and shelling out hundreds of pounds on a single bottle.

But I'm amazed – and frankly delighted – by how many of my colleagues in the wine trade actually seem more interested in finding off-the-beaten-track gems that cost less but still offer great finesse.

I think it's high time some of these fine wine bargains were given more prominence, and here are just some of the wines I've recently been buying and revelling in. (For the latest wine tips, sign up to my free e-bulletin at ollysmith.com).

Alsace is a haven of hidden gems for fine wine lovers. You'll mainly find whites with aromatic qualities there, but on a recent trip I did taste a couple of noteworthy examples of Pinot Noir.

Top producers such as Hugel, Zind- Humbrecht, Ostertag, Kreydenweiss and Trimbach are making white wines of mind blowing quality from grapes such as Riesling, Muscat, Pinot Noir, Pinot Blanc and Gewürztraminer.

In particular, be sure to look for Riesling from prized Grand Cru sites for a white that feels intensely alive with vivid citrus and appley-rich zing.

They are absolutely stunning and a splendid value alternative to wines from other prestigious regions such as France's Burgundy – I've just ordered a few bottles myself.

The red wines of Burgundy, from Volnay to Vosne-Romanée, are considered some of the finest incarnations of Pinot Noir the world over. But with prices often reaching hundreds of pounds a bottle, what are the alternatives?

New Zealand has a good reputation for creating fine Pinot Noir, with Central Otago in particular carving out a niche. – Felton Road makes some truly stonking kit, which you'll find at bbr.com.

In the past it's been relatively affordable for fans of fine New Zealand Pinot Noir, but these days both quality and price are higher.

Beyond Central Otago I've been selecting wines from producers such as Dog Point in Marlborough (available from thewinesociety.com and bbr.com).

But one winery that really catches my eye is Schubert in Martinborough.

As for South America, Chile has long been touted as having great potential for Pinot, and there are still some value options to look out for.

But if it's fine Pinot you're after, have a crack at the outstanding wines of Argentina's Chacra, available from leaandsandeman.co.uk.

If you're a Bordeaux lover, Portugal's Douro has some serious wines that are worth sampling, or you could try the Rhône valley.

And there's always Rioja – a great alternative to classic Bordeaux.

As for Germany, if bright whites are your thing, then revel in the tangerine-like freshness of a good Riesling Kabinett Trocken. With a bit of savvy, fine wines don't have to cost the Earth.

'Extra posh', 'bargain bucket'... even en primeur. Supermarket wine aisles have it all (if you've got a good nose)

Many of us have been tempted by supermarket offers to buy three bottles of wine for £10, or 'buy one, get one free'.

But were these wines ever really going to be sold at their full prices? Was it just a clever piece of marketing to encourage us to buy more wine than we intended? Was the wine really that good?

I believe you can maximise your enjoyment of wine by choosing with a bit of savvy to get great value for money and experience a wider range of tastes.

Today, supermarkets are expanding their online offerings, yet we also have the world in our wine aisles – and you don't need to dig out your passport to explore every exhilarating corner.

Supermarket wines in the UK stand out with their diversity compared to those abroad. Partly it's because our own wine production is so small – in wine producing nations you tend to see mostly local vino.

So, where to buy? Waitrose consistently offers a laudable selection ranging from everyday bargains to seriously fine vino (including Bordeaux en primeur), with delivery free from waitrosewine.com.

In store, you'll find enticing wines from cutting edge regions including Uruguay, Greece, Georgia and Romania.

Meanwhile, Sainsbury's and Tesco are offering entry level own label wines ('House' and 'Simply') as well as fine or more classic wines.

Tesco's Fine Wine selection is evolving online too, having grown to some 300 listings.

The Sainsbury's Taste The Difference range remains solidly impressive, and at the top end they have their Classic Selection, for customers who are dining in or looking for gifts.

Also worthy of praise are the wines of Marks & Spencer – its Italian whites in particular offer stunning value, cleverly blended for simple, crisp refreshment.

Elsewhere, Asda has its Extra Special range and Morrisons has some bankable choices on its shelves too.

But how can you tell what a particular supermarket wine will taste like? Well, wines in supermarkets are usually arranged by country, and there is a rule of thumb you can apply here.

With a hot climate (i.e. somewhere you'd sunbathe), the wines tend to be more generous and fruity in flavour. With cooler climes (for example, northern Europe), expect more zing in the whites and savoury austerity in the reds.

In general, though, my advice would be to keep trying new wines that tickle your fancy.

For me wine is all about fun – new flavours to savour, intriguing textures to consider and memorable nuances to delight in.

And if you're searching for more tips, simply join in the conversation online.

Say cheese! And now ask, white or red?
The choice isn't as simple as you might think…

It's Sunday. You've got the paper open to enjoy a quiet moment and relax with some well earned time to yourself. But now I'm going to shake things up. Ready? Here goes: white wine often pairs better with a cheeseboard than red.

Now, I know that most people adore a glass of red with their cheese – and there are times when that's absolutely the case.

But when you consider the massive range of textures and tastes from blue to Brie, sometimes reds can dominate your carefully selected cheeses where white wines allow a broader range of those flavours to flourish.

When you're matching wine and food, you can complement the flavours (a sweet wine with pudding) or contrast the flavours (a sweet wine with blue cheese).

Generally speaking you want a similar weight of texture in your wine and food – wines range from being light like water to rich and sticky like honey.

Once you've got a balance of textures, you can start to play with the flavours and have some fun – and I'd encourage you to find your own matches made in heaven, however odd they may seem.

Pairing wine with food is all about exploring and expanding the pleasure of mixing and matching different flavours. And you can start very simply. Torn chunks of Mozzarella cheese served with a glass of chilled Prosecco may not sound a likely match, but it's a simple start to a top feast.

At the other end of the flavours spectrum, a chilled glass of Tawny port paired with crumbly Stilton is divine – with complementary intensity, the fruitiness of the wine and the saltiness of the cheese take a happy tumble across the palate and come up smiling, unified and enticing you to dive in for more.

You can experiment pairing the same Stilton with Hungarian Tokaji (I'd go for five Puttonyos, which is at the sweeter end). Or how about Roquefort and Sauternes, which is an absolute classic. (For a bargain, pair Roquefort with Botrytis Semillon from Australia, which is a similar style but generally less pricey.)

With creamy cheeses such as Brie, I'm a fan of white Chardonnay from France's Burgundy. Or consider Chardonnay from Chile.

If you're a red wine devotee, with Brie I'd recommend a lighter grape variety such as Gamay (the grape that makes French Beaujolais). With goat's cheese, white Sauvignon Blanc is a complete treat. Try Sancerre or Sauvignon de Touraine from France's Loire, which can offer some decent value.

However, it's with hard cheese that red wines really come into their own. Mature Cheddar pairs well with well structured Cabernet Sauvignon-based wines such as red Bordeaux.

But just to keep you on your toes, I once paired a powerful Cheddar with a white Fiano from Campania in southern Italy and it was glorious – the intensity of flavours were similarly pitched and the peachy Fiano tamed the turbo-charged oomph of the cheese surprisingly well.

A rule of thumb is to sample local cheese with local wine, for example smelly Époisses with aged red Burgundy (Pinot Noir) or Parmesan cheese with wines made from the Sangiovese grape such as Chianti or Brunello di Montalcino. Or how about experimenting with Cornish Yarg and top notch Cornish fizz?

The world of cheese out there is vast and happily so is the world of wine.

There's some great fun to be had experimenting with pairings to delight guests or just bring an extra dimension to a relaxed evening in front of the telly. The point is to revel in the glory of endless combinations – you may not hit the spot every time but when it works, a wine and cheese marriage can be life-affirming and delightful.

And if you want a simple solution, open two bottles – one red Rioja and one white Chardonnay – with your cheeseboard and encourage your guests to dive in…

Are you a one-trick pony when it comes to wine? My alternative grape guide will have you galloping along

Before working in wine, I used to write for film and TV, specialising in animation. I worked on shows such as *Pingu* and *Charlie And Lola*, and even (for a single day) on *Wallace & Gromit: The Curse Of The Were-Rabbit* – if you wait long enough in the credits, you'll see my name flash past!

Now, in the world of telly and films, we put things into categories: comedy, romance, thriller, western, sci-fi and more. These help us home in on what we might like to watch based on what we enjoy. I want to guide you towards new wines in exactly the same way.

If you send me a message on Twitter or visit my wine bar The Glass House on board the ship Azura, and tell me you love sweet flavours, sharp things like lemon juice, exotic flavours such as lychee, or spicy dishes, or creamy, mellow cheeses, then I can identify a grape variety that'll hit your spot.

You see, grapes each impart a certain character to wine. If you can get a handle on the basics and find one you like, then you can explore more widely and find new wines to savour, share and love. But how exactly should you go about it?

Let's say you're a fan of crisp white wines. Pinot Grigio from Italy and beyond is hugely popular, but there are oodles of other invigorating Italian whites to investigate made from grape varieties such as

Fiano, Falanghina, Verdicchio, Grillo, Pecorino, Greco di Tufo and Grecanico.

Or how about tasting some gloriously fresh Spanish Albariño, or southern French Picpoul de Pinet?

Wines such as these are now widely available, and although each is subtly different, broadly they're all bright, crisp wines that are delicious served chilled as an apéritif or alongside dishes of fish and shellfish.

But what if you're bonkers about the citrus twist of Sauvignon Blanc?

New Zealand has done an amazing job of nailing a popular style of Sauvignon Blanc that delivers a tropical passion fruit tinge.

France tends to produce leaner styles of Sauvignon Blanc such as Sancerre, with more grapefruit-like brightness. South Africa has some stunning appley-fresh examples.

And then there's Chile, which offers a range of styles – generally intense and glittering with laser-like refreshment.

And have you sampled Sauvignon Gris? It tends to be a tad richer than Sauvignon Blanc and offers a similarly intense zing.

If you're a fan of richer styles of white wine such as Chardonnay, how about tasting Chenin Blanc or aged Semillon?

Do you love aromatic whites such as Gewürztraminer? Then have a pop at Argentinian Torrontés.

Looking for more mellow peachy flavours in your white vino? Then embrace the joyful world of Viognier, Marsanne and Roussanne.

For red wine lovers there's an even greater choice. If you enjoy light, easy drinking Beaujolais made from the Gamay grape, I'd recommend checking out Cerasuolo di Vittoria from Sicily or Pinot Noir from South America.

If you're a fan of savoury aged wines like classic Bordeaux, try the widely available Gran Reserva Rioja.

Or say you get your kicks from spicy reds such as Shiraz – in that case, Carmenère from Chile or Touriga Nacional from Portugal are well worth hunting down (you'll find Touriga in many of the blends of the Douro valley).

And if you adore the punchy, bold fruit and spice of famous wines such as Châteauneuf-du-Pape, then the headline grape in the blend is the one to find.

In Châteauneuf that's Grenache, which produces some decent and well priced reds.

The key grape behind red Rioja is Tempranillo, which you can find in the wines of Ribera del Duero. Devotees of Italian Barolo should be searching for the Nebbiolo grape – or you could try Xinomavro from Greece.

And lovers of butch, spicy red Zinfandel from the US would do well to sample the delights of Italian Primitivo.

Wine is a giant network of flavours, and there are numerous points at which the characteristics of certain wines intersect.

Learning about grape varieties and the similarities as well as differences will help steer your choices in the wine aisles towards bottles that build your repertoire – and ensure you discover new treats.

Location, location, location –
when it comes to wine, the terroir is crucial...

The coastal region of Casablanca in Chile is famed for its bright Sauvignon Blanc with fresh, zingy flavours.

The Pacific Ocean acts as a moderating influence, with the Humboldt Current reaching up from Antarctica like a giant air-conditioning unit cooling the coastline.

When visiting Casablanca I've noticed the chill in the air and the blanket of cloud in the morning, which rolls back at midday to reveal bright blue skies.

Just a few miles inland, though, without the cooling clouds, wines are being made with very different characteristics, such as bold, red, fruity Cabernet Sauvignon from the Maipo Valley.

What this illustrates is how the exact location of the vineyard and the climate conditions will have a massive impact on any wine. So when you taste one that you love, make a note of the place it came from and try exploring other vino from that region.

Another hugely important factor, of course, is the winemaking talent involved. But how can you tell what a wine is likely to taste like when you're standing there in the supermarket aisle?

Let's start with climate. In the simplest sense, a vineyard in a hot place will tend to produce boldly flavoured, fruity wines with plenty of alcohol.

Cooler climate vineyards will tend to produce wine with lower alcohol and more acidity. The average temperature of a region can make the difference between a zippy wine such as champagne from northern France and a ripe, bold, red Shiraz from South Africa.

A vineyard's climate will dictate which grape varieties are most likely to thrive there and give you a vital clue as to what kind of wine to expect. I've known reds from high altitudes – such as those of the Uco Valley in Mendoza, Argentina – develop incredible aromas with heady fragrance. The temperatures of coastal vineyards tend to be moderated by the sea, keeping the site warmer in winter and cooler in summer, with the impact on the wine generally being to preserve freshness.

The aspect of a vineyard is also important – a sloping vineyard with a southerly aspect here in the northern hemisphere will get more sun. A slope can also help in a wet place, with water running off the vineyard rather than bogging it down. The reflected luminosity of a river such as the Mosel can also help sloping vineyards further towards ripeness.

Then you've got the soil to think about. Some vineyards are famed for their relationship with the soil they're planted on. For example, the very best Premier and Grand Cru Chablis vineyards tend to be planted on Kimmeridge Clay (also found in Dorset), featuring tiny fossilised shells from the sea.

Many of Bordeaux's fine red wines are made from vines growing on gravelly soils providing good drainage – and you can find wines of great class from New Zealand's Gimblett Gravels.

Some types of soil are better suited to certain grapes than others, and can help in expressing a grape's personality and bringing out its best qualities.

If you really want to explore how a wine's character can be affected by the soil, you could focus on the unique wines of a single vineyard situated on a particularly hallowed piece of ground – for instance, stellar Château Pétrus, with its famous clay, gravel and iron-rich crasse de fer.

Finally, there's the human element to consider. The impact of the individual on winemaking is enormous, from the choice of oak barrels to filtering, selecting different yeasts or deploying techniques such as micro-oxygenation to soften the wine.

Some will intervene more than others, but if you like a certain wine from a particular brand or winery, you should definitely have a crack at further wines from their range.

Every year nature asks a question in a vineyard. Every year winemakers do their best to reply by expressing their ideas through their patch of earth. Wine is a cocktail of tactics, territory, culture, science, intuition and weather.

But above all, winemaking is about belief. It takes guts to try to produce great wine. It can take a lifetime to succeed.

Don't play it cool when it comes to chilling your wine

So you've bought your bottle of wine. You get home with it and what happens to it? Whites in the fridge? Reds in the rack? Watch out!

With our domestic fridges and centrally heated houses we risk exposing wine to extremes of temperature.

Whether you're storing wine for the long term or serving it that very day, to show your wine at its best it's worth taking the temperature.

In summer we perch in our sunny parks and gardens, where our chilled whites get heated to soup in the sunshine. In winter we fire up the central heating to gently roast ourselves for seven months, and our red wines are at risk of being stripped of their aroma, complexity and finesse.

How to get the balance right? In years gone by, houses were cooler and cellars more common, so reds were naturally served a little cooler than they are these days.

Never leave your bottle by the fire or on a radiator; if your red gets too hot you risk stewing it, so it's best to err on the side of caution – and you can always gently warm the glass in your hands if it feels too cool and the aromas are muted.

As a general rule, richer or older reds should be served at around 18°C, whereas lighter and fruitier reds thrive at 14°C and sometimes even lower. In summer I adore light-bodied fruity reds such as Beaujolais or lighter examples of Nero d'Avola from Sicily served gently chilled to bring out their natural fruity exuberance.

Serving whites straight from the fridge can shut down aromas and mute flavours, as domestic fridges tend to be around 4°C.

You want to aim to serve your fizz, whites and rosés chilled rather than very cold, at between 7°C and 10°C. Generally, the wines you buy at supermarkets are designed for immediate drinking, so there's no need to age them for the long term.

For ageing fine wine you need to consider three crucial influences – temperature, humidity and light.

The temperature needs to be constant – ideally 12°C year round – so keep your wine away from radiators and not in, say, sheds or green-houses, where temperatures can fluctuate hugely.

Humidity needs to be monitored so as to prevent the corks from drying out – domestic fridges tend to be very dry, so they aren't the best option for long term storage.

And remember to store the bottles horizontally so the wine is in contact with the cork, to keep it from drying out and letting air get in.

And finally, keep the wine out of direct sunlight and all sources of UV.

If you haven't got a cellar, wine fridges are worth considering, with their accurate, constant control of the environment providing the perfect conditions for your more prized wines to develop over time.

In general, serve your reds slightly cooler than room temperature, and whites chilled but not freezing cold, and you'll be showing off what they've got to the fullest possible extent.

Pop some glorious bubbles
without bursting the bank

Is there such as thing as good value champagne?

If you compare the price of a bottle of champagne for £20 (and more) with the average spend on a bottle of wine, which is less than a fiver, then perhaps not.

But if you compare champagne – with its massive prestige and reputation – with bottles from prized places like Bordeaux where you can pay hundreds if not thousands of pounds for really top vintages, champagne is proportionally far less of a thump in the wallet.

If you're going to get your kicks from wine, it remains a popular hunting ground to swing into the party spirit. But what exactly are you paying for?

The Champagne region is quite far north in France, which means the cool marginal climate varies between great years and poor years, so it can be a risky business.

There's a limit to the land, with around 84,000 acres protected by French law and permitted to use the name champagne.

With growers, cooperatives and champagne houses all dedicated to the art of bubbly, the process of making champagne is lengthy, with a secondary fermentation in every individual bottle.

It takes expertise, finesse, attention to detail and a lot of investment in both time and resources to deliver those tiny tantalising bubbles in every single glass.

With big names such as Bollinger, Roederer, Pol Roger, Lanson and Laurent-Perrier eager to maintain high standards and the prestige of their brands, quality control is a big investment.

Whether it's for a non-vintage champagne that is blended from a number of different years to maintain a consistent house style, or a vintage champagne from a single year that more closely echoes the characteristics of the growing conditions, producers are aiming to stay at the top of the bubbly ladder and fend off the advances of the sparkling wines of New Zealand and even England.

I recently tasted a sparkling wine from Hampshire and I found it thrilling – it's made using the same traditional method as champagne but from a vineyard right here in the UK. The aromas are a stunning whirl of peach and citrus, with a pleasingly tart sherbet-like twist to the palate and zillions of tiny delicate bubbles.

Of course, the price reflects the ambition and quality of this English sparklers, but champagne has a huge range of price points – from great value champagne from vineyard owners such as Hostomme right up to famous prestige cuvées such as Cristal and Dom Pérignon, which can sell for £100 or more.

But some of the best value on the shelves right now comes from supermarket own label champagne. If you're looking for value, they're a great place to kick off the party.

I salute the manager of Morrisons in Seaford who I met while filming for Saturday Kitchen. He was proud to recommend own-label Champagne, which reminded me it's the wine in the bottle that counts.

The choice is yours – and the quality is out there!

The best bred red wine in the world

My taxi driver erupts into a flourish of French insults directed at his sat-nav. No matter how hard he slaps the dashboard, his sat-nav simply doesn't recognise Pétrus – the most legendary name in the wine world.

Connoisseurs crave it, collectors hoard it, investors adore it, Gordon Ramsay named a restaurant after it and I'm on a mission to find out how on earth the sat-nav in a smart modern Mercedes could possibly not know it.

As we finally pull up at Pétrus, the penny drops. Pétrus is about simplicity. No grand château, no landscaped gardens, no fleet of elegant classic cars in the driveway. The main building is compact and Pétrus feels more like a working farm than a castle.

I've dreamt of visiting Pétrus for 17 years, and since visits are extremely rare this is a huge day for me.

And it's memorable not because I've finally been invited to visit a prestigious place whose wines regularly command thousands of pounds for a single bottle (a case of 12 bottles from 1982 is north of £60,000, though you could buy a bottle from 1995 to drink now for around £1,250 and split the cost between a group).

No, this is one of the great days of my life because I learned something I wasn't expecting. Pétrus is not really about names, prices, or prestige. It's about soil.

The vineyard is just 11.5 hectares on a gently rising slope in Pomerol, near Bordeaux, with an altitude of 40 metres. The interplay of Merlot and the unique soil at Pétrus is where the magic happens.

The topsoil of clay is 60–80cm thick and the subsoil is highly dense blue clay, which the roots cannot punch through.

Excess water drains off when it rains, but when it's hot the clay manages to retain sufficient moisture to avoid excess stress to the vines. It's a small miracle of nature.

The day to day mission is to make a wine with as little intervention as possible, to faithfully draw the characteristics of the vintage through the soil and vines into the bottle.

The wine made at Pétrus is a snapshot of the year's mood – and it's thrilling to experience. The 2010 is bright, tight and fragrant with sleek concentration and a twinkle of spice.

The winery is compact and humble, with simple concrete tanks and a glass-lined tank for blending. Its simplicity points to attention to detail.

The grapes are pressed just outside the small winery in a tent. (A new winery is being built but for now the tent was in full swing.) The mood among the handful of people behind Pétrus is workmanlike, focused and understated.

The winemaker is youthful Olivier Berrouet, a young man whose father Jean-Claude before him made wine at Pétrus since 1963. Olivier is more than qualified to take the reins, having worked around the world from France to Argentina.

He is genial, down to earth and offers a refreshingly simple philosophy: 'I would drink any wine from anywhere in the world as long as it has balance.'

After tasting, we briefly talk *Star Wars*, George Lucas and Olivier's delight in the London restaurant scene.

From the roots up, everything at Pétrus is directed towards stewardship of the soil, the wine, the place, the people and the legacy. And for that, a sat-nav is utterly useless.

Simply the zest: Try an alternative to your favourite wine

The popularity of Sauvignon Blanc is legendary. If you're a fan, chances are you're in love with its zingy citrus flavours.

But what if you're in the mood for a change from your usual sip?

Rejoice! For the alternatives at your fingertips are ready to burst out of the bottle.

Picpoul de Pinet remains a huge favourite of mine. Or you can embrace the breezy upbeat crisp wines made from the Albariño grape.

Txakoli from Spain's Basque region has thrusting acidity, and the Grüner Veltliner grape from Austria appeals to lovers of Sauvignon Blanc with a freshness that carries a subtle lacing of white pepper spice.

For another world of wines that pair brilliantly with fish, you could dive in to the treasure trove of Italian whites such as Vermentino or Falanghina.

But you might be surprised to discover another great alternative to Sauvignon Blanc... Chenin Blanc.

It has its spiritual home in France's Loire. There it produces wines that are dry, sweet or sparkling across a range of styles. But in South Africa, Chenin is creating some outstanding examples of invigorating white wine – think Golden Delicious apples fused with a jolt of citrus electricity.

Look for winemakers such as the legendary Ken Forrester, super-talent Bruwer Raats and Adi Badenhorst.

The glory of Chenin is that it is packed with natural acidity, which can produce wines with bright citrus flavours. But thanks to its peachiness and richer texture it can pair successfully with mild aromatic cooking such as stir-fries and curries.

It may never be as widely available as Sauvignon Blanc, but Chenin deserves its day in the sun.

Dinner at your place
(and yes, I'll bring the wine)

You're standing on the doorstep with a bunch of flowers and a bottle of wine, looking forward to catching up with friends over dinner. But as you wait for the door to swing open, a nagging doubt begins to grow. Is the wine in your hand really any good?

Did you spend too much on it – or too little? Will your hosts even bother to open it? Here are some tips to help you pick the right wine at the right price every time.

First, you don't need to spend a fortune to enjoy great wine.

For less than £15 you can choose from a decent range of vino that'll hit the spot.

In general, for £15 or less New Zealand offers some outstanding wines, but I'd also urge you to sample some Portuguese reds, especially from the Douro.

Which brings me to point number two. Consider who you're buying for. Bear in mind that people's tastes in wine can vary enormously. My friend Mark adores savoury aged Bordeaux, but Mark's business partner Nick loves bold, fruity Shiraz. Whenever I have them both round, the safe ground is Rioja. Red Rioja, based on the Tempranillo grape, has a wide appeal to lovers of both classic savoury wines and more fruity, modern styles.

The risk in buying something that you personally can't wait to taste is that the hosts may 'forget' to open it on the night. To avoid this happening, open your bottle at home to allow it to 'breathe' and arrive with it ready to go.

Ideally, contact your host in advance to ask what's on the menu and make an effort to match your wine accordingly. Creamy sauces tend to call for rich oaked whites, spicy curries need wines with some ripe fruit flavours (off dry whites such as Pinot Gris from Alsace work superbly) and roasts are an opportunity to rev up a top quality red.

Venturing off the beaten track can offer you value; or you can play it safe by selecting a bottle of fizz that everyone will love – Prosecco has hitherto been available at great prices, and recently I've noticed some examples of superb quality.

Another thing to consider is how the bottle looks. If you pick a top bottle but the label is torn or looks like it's been daubed by a tipsy chimp, ask your host to decant the wine before serving (decanters look great, but in truth any old jug will do).

Don't, of course, judge a wine solely by its label. While those that are cleanly presented, easy to read and written in plain English may appeal to you, it's no guarantee that the wine inside is any good.

Generally, I wouldn't worry too much about the way the wine looks – just go by taste. And don't feel pressured to spend a fortune.

Happy new cheers: brilliant wines for autumn

Autumn is a buzzing time of year for the wine trade, as suppliers offer a tantalising glimpse of new blends and exciting varieties that'll be available over the next few months.

There are a lot of brilliant new wines coming from southern Europe, and it's exciting to see a renaissance of varieties that have been dormant for too long.

Let's tackle whites first. If you're a fan of crisp zingers such as Sauvignon Blanc, give Vermentino a whirl. A grape found in southern France, Corsica, Italy (where it's also known as Pigato), Sardinia and Australia, it yields wines with breezy, lemony freshness and subtle aromatic fragrance.

Meanwhile, with the success of Spanish Albariño, I'm excited to see exotic, fragrant and inventive blends emerging, with bright aromatic freshness and such delightful fragrance you could dab it behind your ears. Godello is another Spanish white grape coming into fashion that pumps out appley freshness; or you could nab a vibrant Verdejo from Rueda.

Or how about a white Rioja? Alternatively, for a wine that's about as sharp, snappy and searing as they come, try some Txakoli from the Basque country.

As for reds, Portugal is producing some outstanding wines from a whole range of local grapes.

Port producers in the Douro are creating deep and complex dark red blends based on the grape varieties that go into making port, such as Touriga Nacional. If you're a fan of bold, spicy wines such as Shiraz, do check them out.

Elsewhere, it's fantastic to see renewed interest in Carignan, which reminds me of a punkish, butch version of Pinot Noir.

You'll find outstanding examples from old vines in Chile. Or for a bargain, try the Côtes Catalanes appellation in southern France.

Finally, Italy is another haven of splendidly unique reds, and I love the fruity simplicity of Marzemino.

Or there's the juicy, fragrant fun of Nero di Troia, or gluggable value reds made from Nerello Mascalese.

With fabulous new blends and varieties romping onto our shelves, it's the perfect time to dive in and glug for glory.

A pint-pot salute to wine for beer lovers

Though my first love is wine, I'm a big fan of beer as well – I think both drinks offer fascinating differences in flavour depending on where they come from and how they're made.

But what if you're a beer lover taking the first steps into enjoying wine?

Well, a lot of it depends on what type of beer you prefer: light beers such as lagers, richly flavoured beers such as ales and IPAs, or dark, bold, hefty stouts.

Let's start with lager. It's bright, brisk, refreshing and relatively low in alcohol, so my first suggestion would be to step forth into the world of chilled, invigorating white wines.

You don't want anything too heavy, so you'd do well to kick off with Italian whites.

Pinot Grigio is everywhere, but keep your eyes out for northern Italian Pinot Grigio from places such as Trentino; or sample a drop of Fiano from southern Sicily. If it's bubbles you want, have a crack at Italian Prosecco, or else pop a bottle of Spanish cava.

For a sharper kick to your vino, select Sauvignon Blanc with its grapefruit freshness. Tang-tastic!

If you're a fan of fragrant summer ales or the aromatic seduction of Belgian white beers, look for mildly aromatic grape varieties such as Spanish Albariño, apricot-like Viognier or even Argentinian Torrontés for a full on lemon-elderflower assault.

And if you really love your aromatic beer – top notch Hefe-Weiss, say, with its clove and banana niff - you could opt for a glass of Gewürztraminer from Alsace, which will dose you with a vino-hit similar to rose Turkish delight.

Ales are darker, richer and more savoury. Let's talk best bitter, the world of Adnams, Harveys and Otter.

If these traditional brews are your favourites, then I'd suggest sipping some reds from Europe – Rioja is a brilliant place to start. Reds from Rioja tend to be medium bodied with a pleasing savoury hint – and paired up with a slice of Manchego cheese they could almost rival a pint with a ploughman's!

If IPA is more your ticket, especially modern craft beers, then I'd suggest tracking down the pure, fruity, modern wines coming out of Chile and New Zealand.

On the reds front, Chilean Syrah is one to watch – delivering dark fruit with a peppery twist, for me it has huge potential.

New Zealand can also give you a dose of amazing reds, and is massively famous for the verve and passion fruit intensity of its Marlborough Sauvignon Blanc.

But it's seen some exciting diversification too, with whites such as Grüner Veltliner and Pinot Gris shining through.

Finally, there's rich stout. If you're a devotee of the black stuff, then you need to charge your glass with a dose of big, bold red. Italian Amarone or South African or Aussie Shiraz will hit the spot.

Or you could plump for a glass of Pedro Ximénez dessert wine from Spain: very sweet, with dried figs, dates and raisin flavours packed in a syrupy black elixir.

And remember, after a wine tasting there's only one thing for it – a cold glass of beer!

British versus English: what's in a name?

British wine and English wine are two very different things, and it's all too easy to get them confused.

British wine isn't made from grapes grown in Great Britain. It's fermented and bottled on our shores, but the grape juice – often arriving in concentrate form – comes from abroad.

English wine, on the other hand, is made from grapes grown in England. And I'm a massive fan of the rising quality of English sparkling wine in particular.

If you thought English sparkling wine was a novelty, overrated or a blip related to the trend for sourcing locally, you were mistaken. English wine is here to stay. But so, it seems, is British wine.

In the wine trade, mention of the term 'British wine' receives the sort of reaction you'd expect if you said 'muddy puddle'. It's suggested the word 'British' confuses consumers seeking local vino and worse, that it may actually put people off tasting English, Welsh and Channel Island wines.

Nonetheless, British wine's popularity is rising – perhaps thanks to its cheaper price in tough times. But that's not the whole story. Due to producers' attempts to market English sparkling wine better, there are a few different terms for our local fizz knocking around.

There's 'Merret', used by my local winery Ridgeview, paying tribute to Christopher Merret, who presented a paper to the Royal Society in December 1662 documenting how to make sparkling wine – several years before it became famous in the French region of Champagne.

'Cornwall' is used by Camel Valley. And there's 'Britagne' (pronounced 'Britannia'), coined by top class Hampshire fizz outfit Coates & Seely for its new sparkling rosé.

I love the wine, but the word 'Britagne' isn't for me. I'm not convinced we should be looking for words to resonate alongside 'champagne'. I think we ought to embrace the diversity and uniqueness of our own English wines – and for that matter, our wines from Wales and the Channel Islands. Do we really want or need a blanket term?

Of course it would be fantastic to see maximum cooperation from our local wineries in promoting and celebrating our national wines at home and abroad, but I wonder if an all-encompassing term could ever really catch on. Watch this space.

So I'm a big fan of our fizz, and there are some encouraging whites and rosés. I've tasted a few improving reds from our shores, but if I were to suggest one style for you, it would definitely be sparkling – try the wines of Gusbourne, Ridgeview, Camel Valley, Chapel Down and Nyetimber, to name but a few. Perfect for toasting the Queen's Speech at Christmas.

Whatever you do, just don't call it British.

From a glass of fizz at breakfast to a warming nightcap... how to make your Christmas Day go with a splash

The party

Christmas parties rock – but only if the booze lives up to the social buzz! Yet it's really quite simple to get it right if you stick to two golden rules: nothing too fancy and nothing too heavy.

All you really need is some top value fizz to get the party started, followed by white and red wine and a light beer served in bottles from a large bucket of ice.

So first up, the fizz. You can try some Crémant de Jura which is incredible value – it has very brisk bright lemony zip to it and fine bubbles. If you find it a little too brisk, customise it with a jot of blackcurrant cassis, or have a play with cordials such as elderflower or rose.

A white wine has got to be easy and fresh. Pinot Grigio is a safe bet. Or you could branch out into Spanish whites. Less famous, but there are some delicious bargains to be had from the big brand names.

As for a red, you need a light, fruity style – the kind of thing that's perfect for serving at a party – or for making into mulled wine.

The big day

To kick off the day, fizz is essential. I love cracking open an outstanding bottle that pairs beautifully with food – something incredibly rich with a mineral purity to rattle your very soul. Bone dry and with a sense of full throttle power, they should be a bit like holding on to a jet plane as it powers up through the stratosphere.

Or if you haven't done so already, why not try some English sparkling wine?

The feast

With the meal itself, it should be all about excellence. Rioja can be a crowd pleasing alternative to the usual Pinot Noir with turkey, but I'm breaking out into a New World this year. Zinfandel is a treat – or how about Carignan?

If you're keen on a white, Viognier offers a flavour that rings out like a peal of bells – except instead of bells it's the taste of peaches and apricots. Superb stuff, and if you want a dose of the quality kit, look out for French Condrieu – or for a good value option, turn to Chile.

But the white for my Christmas table has got to be the charming balance between richness and elegance of top white Burgundy such as Pernand-Vergelesses – it's a splash out, but compared to some white Burgundies, comparatively good value for money. Wonderful.

The dessert

With pud, a fun frothy contrast with the dense weight of all that life affirming dried fruit is a glass of chilled sparkling Asti Spumante or sparkling Moscato – low in alcohol at around 7.5 per cent, it's an engine rev to the system and gets you back in the mood for hugs and laughter.

But to amp up the Christmas pudding flavours into a maelstrom of rich dark sweetness, seize the tremendous value of Pedro Ximénez sherry. It's black, sweet, rich, sticky and utterly gorgeous.

The cheese board

Cheese at Christmas can only mean Stilton – rejoice! It's the kind of cheese I could roll around in. And it pairs beautifully with a glass of chilled 10 year old Tawny port from Otima – warming, spicy and with a sweet kick it balances and contrasts sensationally with a nibble of Stilton. Remember to serve it chilled.

Afternoon delight

If you're sipping into the late afternoon, the best drink I've found to revive the palate and pick the pace back up is blackcurrant liqueur served lightly chilled. Wonderful and good value too.

Late evening

It's wind down time and you'll be needing a steady sip to savour. I've recently visited the Dalwhinnie distillery and master distiller Bruce introduced me to an absolute treat.

Take a bottle of his light golden bright 15-year-old Dalwhinnie and a couple of tumblers. Put the tumblers and the bottle in the freezer for the day. Open at night and sip for glory. The whisky is gloopy rich and intensely bright with a whirl of upbeat kicks. Pair with dark chocolate for an extra dimension of awesomeness.

Rum can be a splendid top class tipple; I have fallen head over heels in love with Ron Zacapa Centenario Rum Sistema Solera, which is up to 23 years old. It's worth every penny: dense and richly mellow with sweetness and depth, it's a great drink from Guatemala.

Whisky is wondrous but how far have you travelled into the world of specialist distillations? Bruichladdich Organic is amazingly creamy and bright, the kind of drink the Elves themselves probably sip on the eve of battle. This top quality whisky has complex aromas of fudge and mellow brightness whistling out of the glass. It's outrageously creamy and I can't think of many finer ways to celebrate a brilliant British whisky with stunning provenance than to sip it on Christmas Day dressed up as Santa, Rudolf or even the Naughty Christmas Pixie.

And if you want to head to the shops and grab a bottle of classic vintage port, expect dark fruit compote flavours laced with spice – top value.

The nibbles

Here are three wines to pair with mince pies, Christmas cake and all round Christmas flavours.

Rutherglen Muscat: if you see it, buy it, because this stuff runs out at Christmas pronto. You can hunt it from an independent wine shop near you. It is Christmas in a glass – glowing amber with the sweet flavour of raisins and the golden hue of a medal about it. Stunning wine: serve it chilled and marvel.

Old Oloroso sherry: Wow! These wines have been carefully looked after for years and are finally released for your pleasure at an amazing value price. This belongs in your line up because it is world class, a snip at the price and embodies the spirit of Christmas. And look at it this way: if you don't like it, Father Christmas will happily guzzle the lot. It's nut brown, intensely tangy and sweet with a citrus peel kick to the finish that makes you suck your teeth.

A brilliant setting in Portugal's Douro valley is home to a superb operation pumping port – I recommend Quinta do Noval's offerings with gusto. I've even trodden the grapes there myself – a massively memorable and messy experience that resulted in me parading through the premises in my boxer shorts. This is a world of intense dried fruit and nutty flavours with real sweetness and a burst of upbeat spice. Served chilled with a bowl of salted almonds, this to me is the spirit of Christmas. Relax with a glorious glass and share it with those closest to you.

Time to relax the pace with some lighter wines

I'm aware that there are those in Britain who periodically favour abstinence, especially in January, and to those dear friends I say: keep reading, for you'll need these wines when you ease back into the groove.

For the rest of us who reckon that January is the best time of year to enjoy a tipple or two – when the weather's cold, our bank accounts are in hibernation and the sun seems to have been swallowed by a dragon – what's needed are wines that are gentle, lower in alcohol and lighter on their feet than usual.

The key to choosing a wine that's lower in alcohol is generally to avoid the ones that say 'low alcohol' as part of their branding. With a couple of exceptions, in general such wines haven't impressed me with their flavours... yet.

With earlier harvesting, careful selection of clones and the right choice of vineyard site, there are some interesting New Zealand Sauvignon Blancs at just 9.5 per cent alcohol, but in general I prefer styles of wine such as German Riesling or Portuguese Vinho Verde which are naturally lower in alcohol.

If you're looking for a gentler vino, consider wines from cooler regions. Hotter climates encourage grapes to produce more sugar, which converts into higher alcohol during fermentation. Cool climates prevent the grapes from becoming alcoholic time bombs. Northern France is a good place to look – the Loire valley's offerings range from reds and whites to fizz and sweet wines, and are all worth investigating. Italian whites tend to be a good bet too, or coastal Spanish wine such as white Albariño.

Even hot countries have areas of comparative coolness. Try anywhere with a moderating influence – for example, coastal Chile, which has the Humboldt Current in the Pacific coming up from Antarctica, acting like a giant air conditioner for regions such as Leyda and Casablanca.

Argentina has cooler pockets high in the Andes and down in Rio Negro and Patagonia, and is fast developing a reputation for Pinot Noir. In South Africa you've got Elgin, and even warm California has Russian River, which is comparatively cool next to the surrounding areas.

But if you're searching for a region producing wines with moderate alcohol in a properly marginal climate, you need look no further than your local vineyard right here in the UK. English sparkling wine, as my regular readers will know, is close to my heart. I live in Sussex, a stone's throw from several world class fizz producers – Ridgeview, Nyetimber and my very local winery, Breaky Bottom.

Today there are vineyards in England, Wales, Scotland, the Channel Islands and the Republic of Ireland, and you can hunt for the nearest one to you at englishwineproducers.com. The wines they yield are worth investigating for their restrained levels of alcohol and rising levels of quality.

For me, red wines in the UK still have a way to go, but encouragingly decent examples of rosé, crisp whites and fizz have been produced for years. The accolades for English fizz are incredible, including a 2010 Decanter Trophy for the Best Sparkling Wine in the World, and a 2010 International Wine Challenge trophy for Best Sparkling Rosé.

There is, of course, another way to drop the alcohol levels in your wine. By deploying a mixer. I make punch, mulled wine and add fruit cordials and purées to fizz all the time. If you want to add a mixer to your wine, it's your call.

But perhaps the best way of all to lower your alcohol intake is to buy wine that's twice as good and drink half as much of it.

Olly's Winter Warmers –
Recipes to warm your soul

Olly's Mulled Wine
1 bottle red wine
1 cinnamon stick
1 star anise
½ orange studded with 4 cloves
1 vanilla pod halved lengthways
50ml port
100ml orange juice
100g muscovado sugar

Put juice and sugar in a pan, warm until fully blended. Add spices and orange. Leave to infuse for 1 min. Add wine, warm gently for 10 mins. Do not boil. Add the port. Serve warm.

Olly's Winter Warming White
1 bottle fruity white wine
½ slice fresh pineapple (thick cut)
lemon wedge
100g white sugar
1 tbsp runny honey
1 cinnamon stick
100ml pineapple juice

Put juice and sugar into a pan and stir. Warm till blended. Add cinnamon stick, lemon wedge, honey and pineapple and leave to infuse. Add white wine and warm gently for ten mins. Remove orange and spices. Serve warm.

Olly's Tinto De Verano

Red wine
Lemonade
Seasonal fruits
Orange liqueur

Pour equal parts fruity young good value red wine and lemonade into a punchbowl or jug. You could replace the lemonade with fizzy elder-flower. Add heaps of ice cubes. Tip in an abundance of fruit – in winter that means satsumas, oranges and tangerines – along with a good slosh of orange liqueur! Serve liberally.

Olly's Marvellous Mulled Cider

500ml bottle cider
100ml apple juice
1 lemon & ginger tea bag
50ml orange liqueur
1 cinnamon stick
1 heaped tbsp muscovado sugar
½ orange studded with 4 cloves

Put juice and sugar in a pan, warm until blended. Add cinnamon, orange and cider and warm. Add tea bag and infuse for 2 mins; remove. Warm for 10 mins. Stir in orange liqueur. Serve warm.